Retrovisions

Film/Fiction

The Film/Fiction series addresses the developing interface between English and Media studies, in particular the cross-fertilisation of methods and debates applied to analyses of literature, film and popular culture. Not only will this series capitalise upon growing links between departments of English and Media, it will also debate the consequences of the blurring of such disciplinary boundaries.

Editors
Deborah Cartmell – I.Q. Hunter – Imelda Whelehan

Advisory Editor
Tim O'Sullivan

Pulping Fictions: Consuming Culture Across the Literature/Media Divide (1996)

Trash Aesthetics: Popular Culture and its Audience (1997)

Sisterhoods: Across the Literature/Media Divide (1998)

Alien Identities: Exploring Differences in Film and Fiction (1999)

Classics in Film and Fiction (2000)

Anyone interested in proposing contributions to Film/Fiction should contact the editors at the Departments of English and Media Studies, Faculty of Humanities, De Montfort University, Leicester, LE1 9BH, UK.

Film/Fiction volume 6

Retrovisions

Reinventing the Past in Film and Fiction

Edited by
**Deborah Cartmell, I.Q. Hunter,
and Imelda Whelehan**

Pluto Press

LONDON • STERLING, VIRGINIA

First published 2001 by Pluto Press
345 Archway Road, London N6 5AA
and 22883 Quicksilver Drive,
Sterling, VA 20166–2012, USA

www.plutobooks.com

British Library Cataloguing in Publication Data
A catalogue record for this book is available from the British
Library

ISBN 0 7453 1583 6 hbk
ISBN 0 7453 1578 X pbk

Library of Congress Cataloging in Publication Data
applied for

Designed and produced for Pluto Press by
Chase Publishing Services, Fortescue, Sidmouth, EX10 9QG
Typeset from disk by Stanford DTP Services, Northampton
Printed in the European Union by TJ International, England

Contents

Notes on Contributors

Pascale Aebischer is a Research Fellow in English at Darwin College, Cambridge. She has published on Shakespeare and performance theory and is currently working on a book on violence and suffering in Shakespeare's tragedies.

Judith Buchanan is film lecturer in the English Department at the University of York. She works on both Shakespeare and the cinema, separately and in combination. She has written on a number of Shakespearean cinematic adaptations (including the 1899 Beerbohm Tree *King John*, Michael Powell's unmade *Tempest*, Oliver Parker's *Othello* and Peter Greenaway's *Prospero's Books*), and wrote the introductions to three of the Wordsworth Classics composite volumes of Shakespeare's plays: the comedies, classical plays and late plays. Her book *Shakespeare on Film* is forthcoming from Longman in 2002. She also has a book in preparation on Shakespeare on silent film.

Deborah Cartmell is Principal Lecturer in English at De Montfort University. She is co-editor of the Film/Fiction series, co-editor of *Adaptations from Text to Screen, Screen to Text* (Routledge, 1999), *Talking Shakespeare* (Palgrave, 2001) and author of *Interpreting Shakespeare on Screen* (Macmillan, 2000).

Nicholas J. Cull is Professor in American Studies at the University of Leicester, England. He was educated at the University of Leeds and Princeton University, where he held a Harkness Fellowship. He has written widely on issues of film and history, and is the author of *Selling War: British Propaganda and American 'Neutrality' in World War Two* (Oxford, 1995). His current project is a history of the United States Information Agency, 1953–99.

Mark Douglas is lecturer in Cultural Studies at Falmouth College of Arts with research interests in contemporary British and North American culture and media.

I.Q. Hunter is Senior Lecturer in Media Studies at De Montfort University. He is joint editor of Routledge's British Popular Cinema series, for which he edited *British Science Fiction Cinema* (1999), and co-editor of the Film/Fiction series. He is currently finishing a book on Hammer's SF and fantasy films, and preparing one on Paul Verhoeven.

Elizabeth Klett is a PhD candidate in the Department of English at the University of Illinois at Urbana-Champaign. She holds an MA in Shakespeare

Studies from the Shakespeare Institute in Stratford-upon-Avon, and is currently writing her dissertation on contemporary women's performances of male Shakespearean roles.

Barbara Korte is Professor of English Literature at Tübingen University, Germany. Her recent book publications include *Body Language in Literature* (University of Toronto Press, 1997); *English Travel Writing* (Macmillan, 2000), and, as editor, *Many Voices – Many Cultures: Multicultural British Short Stories* (Reclam, 1997), *Unity in Diversity Revisited? British Literature and Culture in the 1990s* (Narr, 1998) and *Anthologies of British Poetry: Critical Perspectives from Literary and Cultural Studies* (Rodopi, 2000).

Stephen Longstaffe lectures in the English and Drama department at St Martin's College, Lancaster, specialising in the drama of the early modern period and twentieth-century popular fiction.

Maria F. Magro is a lecturer in English with Media Studies at Falmouth College of Arts. She specialises in early modern cultural studies and contemporary film. She is completing her doctoral dissertation on early modern authorial subjectivities at Carnegie Mellon University.

Kara McKechnie is a Lecturer in Dramaturgy (Theatre Studies) at Bretton Hall College in West Yorkshire. She has worked at Heidelberg University, Germany and at De Montfort University, Leicester, where she is also completing a PhD on the works of Alan Bennett.

Sarah Neely is a PhD candidate in the Department of Theatre, Film and Television and the Department of English Literature at the University of Glasgow researching the adaptation of contemporary Scottish and Irish literature to film. Originally from the United States, she received a BA from the University of Iowa and an MPhil in Creative Writing from the University of Glasgow.

Renée Pigeon is Professor of English at California State University, San Bernardino. She has written on Sidney, Shakespeare and Elizabeth I, and recently edited a seventeenth-century romance, *Theophania* (Dovehouse Editions). In addition to early modern literature, her research interests include film and detective fiction.

Imelda Whelehan is Principal Lecturer in English at De Montfort University. She is co-editor of the Film/Fiction series, co-editor of *Adaptations from Text to Screen, Screen to Text* (Routledge, 1999), author of *Modern Feminist Thought* (Edinburgh University Press, 1995), and *Overloaded: Popular Culture and the Future of Feminism* (Women's Press, 2000).

1

Introduction: Retrovisions: Historical Makeovers in Film and Literature

Deborah Cartmell and I.Q. Hunter

How can we ever know and accurately represent the past? Laurence Lerner has pointed out that 'it has become a commonplace to argue that history cannot give us direct access to objective facts, since the ideology and the verbal strategies of the historian will determine what he chooses to notice and how he describes it, to say nothing of the connections between events that he then establishes'.[1] This is true of course. Aesthetics and ideology shape our perception of the past, and transform raw facts into stories with causation and meaning. Historians, and historically minded critics, have little choice but to draw more or less consciously on the methods of fiction as well as science. At the same time, the understanding of the past by non-historians – 'ordinary people' if you like – is predetermined by its representation in film and fiction: the French Revolution is inextricable from *A Tale of Two Cities*, the Vietnam War from *Apocalypse Now* (1979). Oscar Wilde remarked that there was no fog in London till the Impressionists painted it. In the same spirit we might say that history is the invention of creative artists as much as an objective record of true events.

The postmodern emphasis on history's construction and textuality is, in many respects, unsurprising. On the one hand, it acknowledges that numerous incommensurable stories can be made up about the past, stories whose truth may be judged according to political usefulness rather than coincidence with reality. On the other hand, postmodern history reflects the general drift nowadays towards cultural and epistemological relativism. Indeed such is the prestige of relativism, and the moral force of the politics of difference, that not only history but truth and, for enthusiastic postmodernists, even reality itself, are declared ideological constructions. 'True perception', we are told, is strictly contingent on the perceiver's social position and lived experience. Declaring one version of history true, from this perspective, is a strategic ploy to create a subversive countermyth about the past.

We came up with the word 'retrovision' to describe how some recent films and novels construct such countermyths. The films discussed in this book demythologise the past, gazing back sometimes with horror at its violence and oppression (the dirt and brutality of the Tudors in *Elizabeth*, the slaughter of *Culloden*) – and sometimes with nostalgia for lost innocence and style (*Cruel Intentions*, *The Avengers*). Taking for granted that the past, like everything else, comes to us by way of previous texts and culturally bounded aesthetic categories, they self-consciously interpret history through the meshes of genre and fictional precedent – *Elizabeth* (1998), for instance, is *The Godfather* in ruffs and hose. In that sense they are both postmodern as academics understand the term – allusive, ironic, knowingly intertextual – and firmly in the line of popular culture's playful and opportunistic treatment of history. Films, to the despair of historians, have always taken a 'postmodern' approach to the past, viewing it not as a dull chronicle but as a dynamic resource for exciting stories and poetic, morally uplifting untruths.

These films' take on history is often subtle and valuable, neither simply a dumbing-down by the popular imagination nor the evacuation of history's meaning in an appeal to a mass audience. Inevitably, perhaps, they see history through the lens of the individual. Although academic history has typically shown the individual dwarfed by the vast, blind and relentless machinery of historical processes, popular film and literature assert that people energetically influence history. The keynote is sounded in *The Terminator* (1984): 'The future is not set. There is no fate but what we make for ourselves.' Interestingly, the renewed popularity of historical film in the last few years echoes the re-evaluation in academia of traditional humanist approaches to history. As faith in grand historical narratives has declined, there has been a revival of biography and narrative history as primary ways of organising the past. Against the post-Foucauldian belief in individuals as faceless creatures of social forces, these, equally postmodern, styles of telling humanise the past, and rescue the agency of individuals from the enormous condescension of those who see only the tidal movements of classes, genders and nations, and the working-out of vast historical processes. Postmodern through and through, historians like Simon Schama see history as 'textualised', shaped by aesthetic principles and read like a thickly descriptive book. But they recognise, too, that the only patterns in history are those imposed by literary skill. Like the New Historicists, they know that every narrative of history is also a discourse of power, but go beyond the monotonous repetitions of New Historicism and its predictable Gothic dialectic of subversion and repression, which, like Dickens's Fat Boy, aims chiefly to make your flesh creep. As Richard J. Evans remarks, postmodern history

> has shifted the emphasis in historical writing ... back from social-scientific to literary models, and in so doing has begun to make it more accessible to the public outside the universities (and indeed to students within them). It has restored individual human beings to history, where social science approaches had more or less written them out.[2]

Readers of this book will see at once that it is dominated by films about the Renaissance and the Jacobean period. The recent burst of films and biographies about Elizabeth I and Shakespeare doubtless reflects both a British desire to revisit history in the wake of new definitions of Britishness and a need to rethink the meaning of Englishness in a devolved nation now that England's myths have been degraded by revisionism. This volume kicks off with Renée Pigeon's '"No Man's Elizabeth": the Virgin Queen in Recent Films', which surveys the current obsession with portraying Elizabeth I on film. Pigeon evaluates *Elizabeth*'s shift in perspective from Elizabeth's usual portrayal as ageing monarch to a youthful and sexually active Queen. The theme of 'uneasy lies the head that wears a crown' is discussed in terms of the way Elizabeth is made 'human', largely through the representation of emotions and sexual urges that she will ultimately abandon in order to become the icon of monarchy in the form of the Protestant equivalent of the Virgin Mother. Similarly, John Madden's *Shakespeare in Love* (1998) addresses this tension between historical/impersonal icon and identifiable 'human' in its juxtaposition of the demands of individual choices in romantic love and the historical reality of arranged matches in the early modern period. *Shakespeare in Love* boldly re-invents the notoriously invisible figure we call 'Shakespeare' into a fully fleshed-out human being – albeit one remarkably like a screenwriter of contemporary Hollywood.

In '*Shakespeare in Love* and the End(s) of History' Elizabeth Klett looks at the double vision of Madden's film. While favouring an ahistorical approach, the film satirises it at the same time. Rather than approving Harold Bloom's argument that Shakespeare single-handedly invented the human, 'personality ... is a Shakespearean invention, and is not only Shakespeare's greatest originality but also the authentic cause of his perpetual pervasiveness' (Bloom's best-seller coincidentally came out at the same time as the film),[3] Klett shows how the film re-invents Shakespeare as a human while problematising historical representation. The film re-establishes a romantic idea of authorship inspired by an extravagantly passionate and, importantly, heterosexual relationship. Both these films thematicise what Stephen Greenblatt has called 'Renaissance self-fashioning', the cultural fashioning of the subjectivity of human beings.[4] They show how 'great' men and women become figures of historical myth, characters in a national epic. At the end of *Elizabeth*, the Queen transforms herself from a human being into Gloriana, the Virgin Queen – a figure we can no longer identify with but who has merged with, raised herself above, history.

Two chapters follow which analyse how contemporary films stifle the radical potential of Shakespeare's plays and conform them to reactionary definitions of gender and race. Maria F. Magro and Mark Douglas look at Trevor Nunn's *Twelfth Night* (1996), which, they contend, closes down the radical possibilities for gender identification and sexuality inherent in the cross-dressing of Shakespeare's play. Similarly, Pascale Aebischer in 'Black Rams Tupping White Ewes: Race vs. Gender in the Final Scenes of Six *Othellos*' analyses the differing portrayals of race in Shakespeare's *Othello*. Most recently, *O* (2000), the teenpic version of *Othello*, even more blatantly closes down the radical potential of its source. Neither of these chapters claims to get at the truth of the play, but explores the different possibilities for staging its contradictions and radical potential.

Currently, teenpic adaptations of the 'classics' seem to be all the rage. Sarah Neely's chapter considers the remake of Choderlos de Laclos's *Les Liaisons dangereuses*, Robert Kumble's 1999 film *Cruel Intentions*. She notes that the recent teenpic film adaptations *Clueless* (1995), *10 Things I Hate About You* (1999) and *Cruel Intentions* (1999) frequently feature, like Shakespeare's plays, a motherless world tenuously ruled by fathers. As well as arguing that this is a symptom of popular culture's anti-feminism, Neely draws attention to these films' thematicisation of the 'makeover': the process of adaptation applies equally to the female characters as they emerge from ugly ducklings into swans (just as the original classic texts are 'made over' into contemporary genre films).

None of these films is stylistically audacious. They all belong to familiar genres, which arguably stifles their radical potential. Peter Watkins's 1964 BBC film of the Battle of Culloden, however, challenges both national mythmaking and dominant media narratives. Rather than look to Hollywood for inspiration, Watkins drew on the techniques of television news and the live broadcast. Nicholas J. Cull's chapter on *Culloden* considers how Watkins challenges Britain's 'reluctance to look boldly and without fear at one's national history'.[5] The result is both vivid immediacy and a dislocating sense of anachronism, which, in Brechtian style, ensures the viewer never forgets the constructedness of the film and, by implication, of every historical narrative. Yet because of its radical, emphatically anti-Hollywood style, *Culloden* has had limited influence on the historical film, which prefers costume drama to hard-edged political deconstructions.

Kara McKechnie contends, however, that even some seemingly conventional and Hollywood-driven representations of the monarchy have an oppositional edge. Taking a synoptic perspective on *The Madness of King George* (1994) and *Mrs Brown* (1997), she examines the current revival of the practice of demythologising monarchs on screen. The seemingly insatiable public need for seeing royals as all too human is seen against a background of history-making; in *The Madness of King George*, the monarch is literally dehumanised by his spin doctors – his individuality is simultaneously invoked and destroyed as he is physically forced into a restraining chair, an ironic image of the throne.

Commercially successful historical films tend to stick to a pattern clearly at odds with what academia knows as 'history'. These patternings are traced by Barbara Korte in her chapter on representations of the Great War in fiction and film as mythologising history, in which she describes how fictional representations rework and seek solace in Christian imagery – soldiers' martyrdom, Christ's Passion, biblical allusions to Cain and Abel, the Apocalypse and the Book of Job. Dwelling exclusively on the 1990s, Korte notes that the most prominent theme in these works is just how the war *can* be remembered, and how these novels and films self-consciously present themselves as 'makeovers', revising our understanding of the war by reworking fictional representations of it.

This theme of the 'makeover' is crucial to an appreciation of films such as *Star Trek, The Brady Bunch Movie, Mission: Impossible* or *The Avengers*, which cash in on a nostalgia for an original TV series. The film adaptation of the television series *The Avengers* (1999) (by no means a success) makes over what Stephen Longstaffe, in the next chapter, argues was always a makeover. The television series' success, he remarks, was due to the way it knowingly adapted, absorbed, parodied and alluded to other films and TV programmes. Like the other films discussed, *The Avengers*, in revisiting the 1960s by way of one of its most characteristic texts, calls attention to its fabrication of a sense of the past. But the England it constructs is entirely imaginary and surreal – the film is nostalgic for the style of the 1960s rather than for the 60s themselves – and very different from the 'heritage films' of Merchant–Ivory, in which England's past is ossified as glamorous spectacle. The *Avengers* film includes not only globally recognised signifiers of Englishness, but also Anglophile in-jokes and pleasurably gratuitous references to the children's literature that has been so crucial to England's self-invention. The result is therefore oddly true to the retrovision of the original TV series, whose early postmodern style it intensifies and parodies. But like *The Last Action Hero* (1993) the film turned out to be too postmodern for its own good.

In the final chapter, Judith Buchanan goes back to the future, so to speak, and considers different critical perceptions between the 1950s and the present day. While it is a common practice nowadays to recognise and publicise a film as an adaptation, when Fred McLeod Wilcox was promoting *Forbidden Planet* (1956), the opposite was the case. Buchanan notes how the film was publicised in terms of its newness and dazzling special effects, and that none of the contemporary reviews mentioned its possible famous literary source. Critics were struck by its uniqueness within the SF genre rather than its makeover of Shakespeare's *Tempest*. Now it is its proximity to a canonical Renaissance text (a proximity that might only be incidental) which critics almost always make the centre of their interpretation.

The volume begins and ends with the English Renaissance, a time when the individual, who rises into prominence as artist, is at the same time 'self-fashioned', to use Greenblatt's word, and is thus unknowable or inaccessible. According to Greenblatt, this period appeals to us today because it represents the early, tentative fashioning of modern consciousness: 'we continue to see in the Renaissance the shaping of crucial aspects of our sense of self and society and the natural world, but we have become uneasy about our whole way of constituting reality'.[6] The films discussed in this volume address, to varying degrees, this conflict between 'the King's two bodies', the private and the public, the individual and society, 'reality' and representation, a conflict very much alive in lit. crit. circles (the Romantic humanism of Harold Bloom versus the hard-bitten Stephen Greenblatt). Some of these films return to one of the great myths of women's literature, the Cinderella story, the fantasy of the makeover. In essence, that is what all the films included in *Retrovisions* are: re-fashioning or makeovers of history.

Notes

1. Laurence Lerner, *The Frontiers of Literature* (1988), reprinted in Dennis Walder (ed.), *Literature in the Modern World* (Oxford: Oxford University Press, 1990), p. 334.
2. Richard J. Evans, *In Defence of History* (London: Granta Books, 1997), p. 248.
3. Harold Bloom, *Shakespeare: the invention of the human* (1998 rpt.; London: Fourth Estate Limited, 1999).
4. Stephen Greenblatt, *Renaissance Self-Fashioning: from More to Shakespeare* (1980; rpt. Chicago and London: University of Chicago Press, 1984).
5. Nicholas Cull, this volume.
6. Greenblatt, *Renaissance Self-Fashioning*, p. 74.

2

'No Man's Elizabeth': The Virgin Queen in Recent Films

Renée Pigeon

No viewer interested in the intersection of film and history will be surprised that the most recent film about Queen Elizabeth I, 1998's *Elizabeth*, is historically inaccurate, featuring invented or grossly misrepresented events and characters. Inaccuracy has of course been the rule rather than the exception in historical films and, as Robert Rosenstone among others has vigorously and persuasively argued, should not be a primary concern in responding to them:

> Both the dramatic film and the documentary are forms for creating a visual past. Both are subject to (at least) two kinds of limitations: the possibilities of the medium and the practices acceptable to audiences in a particular time and place. This ... is equally true of historical writing ... our task is to learn to judge films by their own rules of engagement with the past.[1]

The makers of *Elizabeth*, moreover, expressed no interest in historical veracity, disclaiming any allegiance to fact with unusual vehemence. My intent in this chapter, however, is not to enumerate the many inaccuracies of *Elizabeth* but rather to examine how the representation of the Tudor queen in this recent 'biopic', and in her two much briefer appearances in *Orlando* (1992) and *Shakespeare in Love* (1998), corresponds with or challenges the conventional construction of Elizabeth's popular image.

In depicting Elizabeth I in twentieth-century film and video, filmmakers have embraced certain conventions associated with her representation which first arose during her own lifetime and shortly after her death, as her popular image began to take shape. First and foremost among these has been the notion that she sacrificed the 'natural' destiny of a woman, marriage and children, trading personal happiness for public power. The centrality of this concept to

Elizabeth's popular image as the 'Virgin Queen', and speculation about what motivated her lifelong single state, long predate her cinematic portraits. Various motivations for Elizabeth's resistance to marriage have been considered in turn by her contemporaries, by later historians, and by a host of authors (playwrights and screen-writers among them), who have fictionalised her life during the last four centuries and contributed to the formation of her popular image.

Although Susan Doran has recently argued that 'there is no strong evidence that Elizabeth ever did make a commitment to remain single',[2] Carole Levin summarises the view of many historians when she notes that Elizabeth's failure to marry had 'considerable merit' as a political strategy:

> Unmarried, Elizabeth avoided the role of wife and the risk of being perceived as the inferior partner in the marriage relationship. Also, she need worry neither about lack of fertility and subsequent embarrassment, such as dogged her sister Mary, nor about the risks of dying of disease related to childbirth, as were the fates of two of her stepmothers, Jane Seymour and Katherine Parr.[3]

A contrasting notion, that Elizabeth rejected marriage not as an intentional political tactic but because of personal demons, found its most influential expression in Lytton Strachey's *Elizabeth and Essex: A Tragic History* (1928). As Barbara Hodgdon notes, Strachey 'puts the queen on the analyst's couch'.[4] He sees Elizabeth as irrevocably marred by the traumas of her childhood – the brutality of her father, the execution of her mother – and thus physically incapable of normal sexual relations:

> A deeply seated repugnance to the crucial act of intercourse may produce, when the possibility of it approaches, a condition of hysterical convulsion, accompanied, in certain cases, by intense pain. Everything points to the conclusion that such – the result of the profound psychological disturbances of her childhood – was the state of Elizabeth.[5]

Strachey's interpretation, though challenged by historians,[6] has so influenced the popular image of Elizabeth that a version of it even surfaces in a recent biography written for children, which asserts that she 'grew up afraid to trust anyone' and that her fear of marriage 'ruled the queen of England as strongly as she ruled her country'.[7]

And his psychobiographical approach certainly coloured the cinematic representation of Elizabeth, since *Elizabeth and Essex* became Maxwell Andersen's source for *Elizabeth the Queen*, the play that in turn was the basis for *The Private Lives of Elizabeth and Essex* (1939) and Bette Davis's memorably neurotic portrayal of the queen.[8]

Although Elizabeth's reign lasted 45 years, the popular image of both the queen and the Elizabethan period belongs to the last ten or fifteen years of that reign, from the late 1580s to her death in 1603 – a period that includes the defeat of the Spanish Armada, Shakespeare's rise to prominence as a playwright, and the publication of Spenser's *Faerie Queene*. Like Queen Victoria, in her popular embodiment Elizabeth has seldom been depicted as a young woman. As Roy Strong notes, even during her lifetime her portraits depicted the mature queen, finally becoming 'spectacular bejewelled icons ... which managed to totally obliterate any memory and ultimately any recognition of those early portraits in which she appears as something approximating to a human being'.[9] Her representation on film and video does feature a few exceptions to this convention – for example, Jean Simmons in *Young Bess* (1953) or Glenda Jackson's extended portrayal in *Elizabeth R* – but the dominant visual image of Elizabeth, first in her portraits and later in film, has been the queen in the latter half of her reign.[10]

The image of an ageing Elizabeth in turn raises the issue of her response to the loss of her youth, and just as she has been conventionally represented as having sacrificed love and family, so too has she often been imagined as unable to accept the passing of time with grace and dignity, becoming embittered as the years passed. This aspect of the queen's popular image has its roots in the panegyric that evolved at the Elizabethan court, where by the 1590s young courtiers 'sought the queen's favors with formulaic expressions of love and wonder, and compared Elizabeth, then in her sixties, to Venus'.[11] The government also attempted during that decade to control the likenesses of Elizabeth by authorising Nicholas Hilliard's so-called 'Mask of Youth' as the only official image of the queen in order to avoid realistic depictions of her as increasingly elderly, and freeze her at mid-life, neither young nor old, but a symbol of perpetual power. As Strong acknowledges, however, this policy of 'deliberate rejuvenation ... may not have reflected vanity so much as a genuine fear of the dangers inherent in dwelling on the physical mortality of the sovereign when the succession was unsettled'.[12] Similarly, the panegyric expressed by poets such as Ralegh and

Elizabeth's response to it involve the complex interactions of Elizabeth's authority over her court and the young men who peopled it, often chafing in private at their subordination to female power while they publicly lauded the queen.

But these caveats aside, the popular image paints Elizabeth in the last years of her life as unwilling to acknowledge the passing of time, still hungry for the insincere flattery of her young courtiers. This motif of the queen's anxiety over ageing most often takes the form of a confrontation between Elizabeth and her mirror: for example, Flora Robson portrays her in *Fire Over England* (1937) as wearily contemplating her reflection and contrasting it to the youthful beauty of one of her ladies-in-waiting.[13] While historical analysis certainly casts some doubt on the validity of this popular image, it is this vain, elderly queen who figures in Virginia Woolf's *Orlando*, and whom Quentin Crisp portrays in Sally Potter's 1993 film.

Both the text and the film of *Orlando* raise interesting questions about gender and its construction;[14] however, Woolf's characterisation of the queen, followed quite closely by writer-director Potter in her screenplay, in many ways reiterates elements of the conventional image of Elizabeth. Woolf employs synecdoche to depict Orlando's first view of the queen, an image transferred very directly to Potter's film version:

> Such was his shyness that he saw no more of her than her ringed hand in water; but it was enough. It was a memorable hand; a thin hand with long fingers always curling as if round orb or sceptre; a nervous, crabbed, sickly hand; a commanding hand; a hand that had only to raise itself for a head to fall; a hand, he guessed, attached to an old body that smelt like a cupboard in which furs are kept in camphor; which body was yet caparisoned in all sorts of brocades and gems; and held itself very upright though perhaps in pain from sciatica; and never flinched though strung together by a thousand fears; and the Queen's eyes were light yellow.[15]

Through this description of the royal hand, Woolf evokes the contrasting images of the queen's two bodies, the body politic and the body natural: the hand that can command, can hold a sceptre, but which now belongs to the failing body of an elderly woman.

Potter adapts Woolf's lyrical musing on the nature of the Elizabethan age – 'Everything was different ... The rain fell vehemently or not at all. The sun blazed or there was darkness.

Translating this to the spiritual regions as their wont is, the poets sang beautifully how roses fade and petals fall'[16] – by giving Orlando a passage from Book II of Spenser's *Faerie Queene* to recite in his first nervous appearance before the queen:

> Ah, see the virgin Rose, how sweetly she
> Doth first peep forth with bashful modesty,
> That fairer seems, the less ye see her may;
> Lo, see soon after, how more bold and free
> Her bared bosom she doth broad display;
> Lo, see soon after, how she fades and falls away.[17]

But Elizabeth interrupts him to ask, 'Is this a worthy topic from one so clearly in the bloom of youth to one who would desire it still?' Orlando's father rises to make a stuttering attempt to excuse his son's *faux pas*: 'Fair Virgo! your – ahem – *bloom* is legendary!' In the casting of Quentin Crisp as Elizabeth in *Orlando*, mask overlaps mask: Crisp, the elderly 'queen', plays the elderly Queen Elizabeth, male masquerading as female in his performance as age masqueraded as youth in Elizabeth's public iconography in the latter years of her reign; and as Sharon Ouditt notes, 'A man acts the part of a woman who was known to play the part of a prince.'[18] The transparent preposterousness of the compliments Orlando's father offers to the queen are underscored by the Spenserian text Potter has selected for Orlando to recite: not merely a classic evocation of the 'carpe diem' (or 'carpe florem') theme, it is the song sung in the Bower of Bliss, the haunt of the seductive witch Acrasia. The next stanza continues the song:

> So passeth in the passing of a day
> Of mortal life the leaf, the bud, the flower,
> Ne more doth flourish after first decay
> That erst was sought to deck both bed and bower
> Of many a lady and many a paramour:
> Gather therefore the Rose, whilst yet is prime,
> For soon comes age, that will her pride deflower ... [19]

An interesting intertexuality is at play here. Through her selection from Spenser, Sally Potter recalls not the flattering figure of Gloriana, the 'Faerie Queene' of the poem's title whom Spenser acknowledges as an image of Elizabeth, but instead the dangerous figure of Acrasia, whose lust saps and ultimately destroys her lovers. The 'carpe florem' motif's focus on mortality in turn focuses attention on Elizabeth's advanced age. Her desire for the young Orlando, whose androgynous nature she recognises[20] parodies Acrasia's enchantment of her lover, Verdant:

> There, whence that Musick seemed heard to bee,
> Was the faire Witch her selfe now solacing,
> With a new lover, whom through sorceree
> And witchcraft, she from farre did thither bring
> There she had him now layd a slombering,
> In secret shade, after long wanton ioyes:
> Whilst round about them pleasauntly did sing
> Many faire ladies, and lascivious boyes,
> That ever mixt their song with light licentious toyes.[21]

Potter extends the image of Elizabeth as a parody of Acrasia by making her responsible for a kind of sorcery in granting Orlando's immortality (in Woolf's original, Orlando simply falls inexplicably into periodic trances and fails to age). The queen grants him a grand house on one condition: 'Do not fade – do not wither – do not grow old' – freeing Orlando from the fate Elizabeth herself has not been able to escape.

Both Woolf and Potter depict Elizabeth deeply embedded in her iconic role; the film *Elizabeth* undertakes a different project, however, offering one version of the genesis of that familiar image. In contrast to the ageing queen imagined by Woolf and embodied by Crisp in Potter's film, the makers of *Elizabeth* chose to portray her early life, beginning with her precarious situation during the final days of her sister Mary's reign. As noted earlier, they were unusually vocal in claiming that they were not concerned about historical accuracy: costume designer Alexandria Byrne recalls that 'Every time I was reading a reference book ... [director Shekhar Kapur] would tell me to close it and throw it away, because he didn't want us to be tied to the fact and reality of it.'[22] Despite this disdain for 'fact and reality', the film nevertheless achieves a high degree of visual fidelity to the Elizabethan period. Aside from an insufficiently aquiline nose, Cate Blanchett is well cast to physically approximate the young Elizabeth, and some scenes, such as the queen's coronation, are based very directly upon contemporary visual sources. Among *Elizabeth*'s weaknesses, however, is the unfortunate casting of Joseph Fiennes, who lacks an adequately formidable screen presence to play Lord

Robert Dudley convincingly; he appears to much better advantage in another Elizabethan role, as the title character in *Shakespeare in Love* (1998).

In some respects, *Elizabeth* does depart markedly from the conventional representation of the queen: first, by depicting her as a young woman, but more significantly and radically in its representation of her sexuality. The film adheres quite faithfully, however, to another convention by structuring her life as a choice between the seemingly irreconcilable poles of love and duty. As Kapur saw it,

> *Elizabeth* is about the choices that we make. This is basically the dilemma Elizabeth faces as a very young person. What does she have to do to survive? Does she go on being a loving, joyous, caring, tactile human being, or does she cut that out and become an image: a ruthless, powerful monarch, but, inside, just a shell.[23]

Despite *Elizabeth*'s contemporary elements – bisexuality, cross-dressing, graphic violence, and the title character's loss of her celebrated virginity – it remains in many ways a remarkably conventional work, belonging to a genre of 'private histories' that seek to translate the conflicts experienced by historical figures into 'more immediate personal and often psychological terms that are accessible to the audience'.[24] In the case of *Elizabeth*, this consists, as Kapur's remarks suggest, of depicting her devolution from human being to empty husk.

That the decision to have Elizabeth unambiguously consummate her relationship with Robert Dudley was a key element in her characterisation is clear from Kapur's scoffing comments:

> Since Elizabeth's story isn't part of my culture, I wasn't saddled with that automatic reverence for royalty which still keeps the English from being able to see her as a real person. Even now, they're obsessed with the idea of her being a literal virgin – it's like the way they treat the existing Royal Family. As long as they're looking at *her*, they never have to look at *themselves*.[25]

Kapur apparently does not even entertain the possibility that the historical Elizabeth might have been both 'a real person' *and* a 'literal virgin' because this doesn't fit the film's relentlessly modern assumptions about human behaviour, despite the host of dangers, not the least of which was pregnancy, sexual activity might have posed for the queen. The choice to 'deal boldly with the issue of Elizabeth's single most legendary characteristic'[26] stems from the filmmakers' desire, stressed throughout the film's promotional discourse, to avoid what producer Tim Bevan termed the 'Merchant–Ivory approach', or what Kapur characterised as 'some classic period piece full of people in big, stiff clothes moving around on big, stiff sets'.[27] Clearly, they saw their film as a challenge to the romanticising of the past commonly attributed to heritage cinema,[28] particularly the maligned Merchant–Ivory films. But, as Claire Monk has convincingly argued, gender is deeply implicated in the critique of heritage cinema that is echoed throughout the film's promotional materials.[29] The choice of, among other influences, *The Godfather* and the 'conspiracy thriller' as models for *Elizabeth* – decidedly 'male', action-oriented narratives – suggests that the film attempts to 'masculinise' material that viewers might typically expect to receive a different generic treatment. But in any event, the superficial boldness inherent in the film's approach to Elizabeth's character is offset by the diminished image of the queen it ultimately offers.

We first see Elizabeth as a princess during her sister's reign, enveloped in sunlight. Her dependence on Lord Robert Dudley is emphasised not only through the dialogue – he urges her as she is arrested for treason on Mary's order to 'Remember who you are' – but also through an insistent, even heavy-handed use of shot/reverse-shots that show Elizabeth looking to him for approval, and make her the object of his gaze. Early in the film, Blanchett effectively portrays Elizabeth's infatuation with Dudley and her inability to hide it. When Cecil attempts to introduce her to the French ambassador during the celebration of her accession to the throne, the presence of Lord Robert completely distracts her, momentarily capturing her attention, to Cecil's obvious dismay and embarrassment.

The dilemma Elizabeth faces, how to balance the public and the personal, is most clearly evoked in the scene that follows. First, Dudley makes his way into Elizabeth's bedchamber past giggling ladies-in-waiting, who then peek through ornamental stonework to observe the queen and her lover. The arrival of Cecil interrupts their voyeuristic fun, and he instructs them that in the future he will need to see Elizabeth's bed-sheets daily, since 'Her majesty's body and person are no longer her own property. They belong to the state.' As he departs, the camera pans back to Elizabeth's chamber, where she and Dudley make love in a bed hung with sheer curtains imprinted with a curious pattern of eyes and ears. Ironically, this design appears to have been adapted from the 'Rainbow' portrait of Elizabeth, in which she wears an elaborate cloak with this pattern, symbolising her advisors who supply her with the information or 'intelligence' that allows her to rule effectively.[30] The original iconographic force of the image is thus reversed in *Elizabeth*, emphasising instead the insistent surveillance of her most private moments; Cecil will later declare to the queen that she can have no secrets.

In showing Elizabeth heavily dependent upon Dudley and chafing under the restrictions of Cecil's paternal advice, the film quite reasonably suggests that early in her reign she had to move away from a reliance upon those who had been closest to her and struggle to assert her authority over a male hierarchy dubious about her capacity to rule. Casting white-haired Lord Richard Attenborough as Sir William Cecil, who in fact was only 13 years Elizabeth's senior and thus a mere 38 years of age when she ascended the throne, underscores his role in the film as a patriarchal figure from whom the queen must free herself (she eventually does so in one of the film's many inventions, sending him off to retirement with the consolation prize of being named Lord Burghley). The ghost of another overpowering male authority, her father, is evoked when we see her awash in remorse over the death of her young soldiers in Scotland, prostrate in front of Holbein's famous portrait of Henry VIII. Her chief antagonist in the film, the Duke of Norfolk, refers to her disparagingly as 'that heretic girl'. But rather than showing her as genuinely successful in her struggle not only against the men who oppose her but even those who support her, and despite her assertion to Cecil that 'from this moment I shall follow my own opinion', ultimately she simply exchanges authority figures, eventually replacing Dudley and Cecil with Walsingham. Even her confrontation with Parliament over the Act of Uniformity – the scene in the film that best suggests the historical Elizabeth's skilfully politic manipulation of her power – is undercut by the revelation that she won the day by five votes because Walsingham temporarily imprisoned six of the opposing bishops.[31]

If Elizabeth faces opposition and possible betrayal in her initial attempts to find her political footing, other conflicts also beset her. The film reiterates Lytton Strachey's vision of a queen bedevilled by psychosexual anxieties by externalising those fears. While Elizabeth does takes Dudley as her lover at least briefly, in a scene employing the kind of 'mainstream eroticism ... which narrows sexuality and sensuality to soft-core sex acts',[32] other images of sexuality and sensuality are threatening or deadly. Mary of Guise, seen seductively bantering with Walsingham about whether he would prefer to 'get into bed' in an alliance with the French or the Spanish, is found naked in her bed the following morning, dead from poison. One of Elizabeth's ladies-in-waiting, Isabel Knollys, seduced by the frustrated Dudley as a surrogate for Elizabeth because of his estrangement from the queen, turns during their assignation from orgasmic cries to screams of terror: the dress she is wearing, borrowed without the queen's knowledge, was a deadly gift to Elizabeth from Mary of Guise. Nor are women the only victims: Walsingham calmly cuts the throat of an effeminate young man with whom he appears to have just shared a bed.

Elizabeth herself barely escapes assassination in a scene which, like so many in the film, employs visually sumptuous spectacle. By the light of fireworks and candles, boats bearing the central characters criss-cross the Thames, and Elizabeth and Robert recline on deep red and gold cushions in the stern of a barge, shaded from view by gauzy curtains, idling in their own Bower of Bliss. After reciting Sidney's 'My true love has my heart', Robert asks her to marry him. When Elizabeth laughingly responds, 'On a night such as this could any woman say no?', Dudley presses his point: 'On a night such as this could a *queen* say no?' Elizabeth asks, 'Does not a queen sit under the same stars as any other woman?' But the film's answer to this question is 'of course not', and moments later, after Robert has asked the Spanish ambassador to use his status as a bishop to marry them, an arrow kills one of Elizabeth's guards, quickly followed by a second which barely misses her. The rapidity with which a sensual moment shifts to violence symbolises the dangers faced by Elizabeth if she slackens her self-restraint; the warm reds and golds of the scene, with their evocation of lush sensuality, are transformed into the red of her guard's blood as he falls on top of her. The second arrow imprisons her, writhing and crying out, beneath one of the gauzy curtains, an image both claustrophobic and sexually suggestive.

Frankly, the film offers Elizabeth rather grim alternatives. Sexuality leads to violence and quite possibly death. Under pressure to marry, she can select as her husband a simpering French prince with a private penchant for cross-dressing, or choose to sustain a relationship with an untrustworthy, weak, married lover who betrays her, and who suggests that the solution to their difficulty is for her to wed Philip of Spain, who will permit them to continue their affair.

Not surprisingly, she rejects both of these choices. But how should she rule? By following the model of her repressive sister and entering into a loveless dynastic marriage, or by opting instead for the stance of warrior-queen Mary of Guise, whose unbridled sexuality is the direct cause of her death – the two distinctly negative counter-images of females in power offered in the film?

Caught between the figurative Scylla and Charybdis of Mary Tudor and Mary of Guise, Elizabeth finally takes as her model a third Mary, the Virgin Mother, and turns herself into an icon for her people to adore. Her apotheosis, framed as her renunciation of normal human life, constitutes the film's climax. Kneeling in front of a statue of the Virgin, as Walsingham hovers above her, she asks, 'Am I to be made of stone? Must I be touched by nothing?' His response, 'Ay, Madam, to reign supreme', encapsulates the film's insistence that no vestige of human feeling can survive her transition to ultimate power.

As I noted earlier in this chapter, part of the conventional popular image of Elizabeth has been that she achieved that ultimate power by giving up her 'natural' destiny as a woman. It's often portrayed, certainly, as a bad bargain, one that embitters her; but the choice she makes is to rule rather than to be ruled by any man. Attempting to explain how the woman became the symbol, however, *Elizabeth* shows her transformation encouraged by the Svengali-like influence of Walsingham in the emotional aftermath of Dudley's betrayal. While her conscious decision to become a Protestant alternative to the Virgin dramatises the view of at least some historians about the rise of the 'cult of Elizabeth',[33] her choice is not an astute political strategy but a sacrifice that arises from her own emotional pain, and one that can hardly even be characterised *as* a choice, given her limited alternatives as the film presents them. While the final scene shows Elizabeth's court – Walsingham last of all – kneeling in awe at her metamorphosis, the film gives us an Elizabeth who is diminished by her entrapment inside an inescapable role.

While *Elizabeth* follows many of the conventions associated with the representation of historical figures in the biopic genre as it first developed during the studio era,[34] biopics are of course as dynamic and subject to change as any other genre[35] and several other influences are readily apparent in the film. Producer Tim Bevan thought of it as a 'conspiracy thriller'.[36] The naïve Elizabeth's discovery that her lover Dudley is married is familiar from countless 'woman's films'; when the lovers confront one another, the banal dialogue includes such time-worn lines as Robert's 'You must let me explain' and Elizabeth's 'Do you love her?' The horror film genre surfaces after Elizabeth's decision to send soldiers to Scotland; when her flowing hair is first restrained in a more elaborate style (foreshadowing its cropping in the film's climax), lightning flashes and the soundtrack reverberates with heavy-handed chants. Several critics noticed what Bevan confirmed, that a film about a family rather different from the Tudors (though at least as dysfunctional) was a primary source: Richard Alleva remarks that 'I don't know which historians director Shekar Kapur and writer Michael Hirst consulted ... but it's quite clear that they must have seen *The Godfather* at least 47 times'.[37]

The influences on the film's depiction of Elizabeth, however, extend beyond its borrowing from a hodgepodge of film genres; underlying the depiction of her eventual entrapment in her iconic role one finds not only the figure of Michael Corleone, but also 'the ghost of Princess Diana'.[38] The Elizabeth of the earlier sequences of the film, a kind of ur-Diana – girlish, impetuous, emotionally needy, and shaken by the sudden demands of her position – seems indebted to the widespread public perception of the late Princess of Wales as an initially innocent young woman destroyed by the role she was required to play, the rigid orthodoxy of the Royal Family, and her husband's betrayal of her. Blanchett's comments on her role acknowledge this connection:

> To become a queen means to erase your past in a lot of ways – look at Diana, her past haunted her, and people wanted to know all about her. But how can you actually rule without a personal self and a personal history? Elizabeth was as much a Maggie Thatcher as a popular Diana. She was able to meld those two things.[39]

But the attempt to meld 'those two things' – the vulnerability of a Diana and the ruthlessness of a Thatcher, a modern counterpart to the queen's body natural and body politic – is inevitably construed as a loss of humanity for Elizabeth in the film.

The burden of rule is an old complaint, one often voiced by Shakespeare's kings: 'What infinite heart's-ease', protests Henry V, 'Must kings neglect that private men enjoy! / And what have kings that privates have not too, / Save ceremony, save general ceremony?'[40] But it is also a topos whose ideological function has been to remind and reassure us that having power isn't truly any fun at all, and that it's much better to be a milkmaid than a princess. In a perceptive review of *Elizabeth*, David Walsh writes that

> Its theses that political power hardens and inevitably dehumanizes an individual, that the decision to sacrifice a satisfying emotional life in the interests of the state and the nation is a harsh one, that everyone perhaps – in one way or another – makes difficult choices to survive and pays the price for those choices, are not terribly original ideas, nor, perhaps more importantly, presented in a particularly fresh fashion.[41]

A film that convincingly depicted how the young queen was able to remain 'no man's Elizabeth', to insist against all the weighty tradition of female subordination in the sixteenth century and the expectations of her advisers and people that she would have 'one mistress here and no master', would be well worth watching, especially with Cate Blanchett in the central role. It's the conventionality of *Elizabeth*, the banality of the queen it constructs, rather than her questionable historical validity, that make it a far less interesting film than it might otherwise have been and that leave open the question of whether it's possible to portray Elizabeth I in a manner that challenges not only the stale conventions of her popular image, but the equally hoary representation of the price of power and fame.

Before concluding this chapter, I'd like to turn to another image of Elizabeth I offered to filmgoers in 1998, Judi Dench's performance in *Shakespeare in Love*, for at least a partial answer to that question. Although like *Orlando*'s Elizabeth she has lost the 'bloom of youth', Dench's queen seems to accept who and what she is, demonstrating a dour, sharp-eyed awareness of her obsequious courtiers' ambitions, and, quite simply, more intelligence than any other character in the film. It's not surprising that a screenplay in which Shakespeare calls the first draft of his new play 'Romeo and Ethel, the Pirate's Daughter' also has fun with the conventional representation of Elizabeth; for example, Wessex stresses to Viola's nurse that 'The Queen, Gloriana Regina, God's Chosen Vessel, the Radiant One, who shines her light on us, is at Greenwich today ... and if we're late for lunch, the old boot will not forgive.' In a marvellous final exit that plays with one of the best-known images of Elizabethan chivalry, the queen's courtiers stand by a puddle a moment too long; when they suddenly recognise what's expected of them, a flurry of cloaks descend as the queen splashes her way to her carriage, muttering, 'Too late, too late.'

But Elizabeth's popular image as the Virgin Queen also serves as a counterpoint to the film's central action, the love of Will and Viola and the barriers that impede them. In her brief appearance, Dench manages (with the assistance of Norman and Stoppard's witty script) to suggest Elizabeth's own past through the sympathy she expresses for Viola's plight. She acts as a *dea ex machina* in the film's climax, but one whose power does not extend far enough to rescue Viola from her marriage to the boorish Wessex: 'How is this to end?' he asks, his bride still dressed as a boy actor. 'As stories must when love's denied,' replies Elizabeth, 'with tears and a journey. Those whom God has joined in marriage, not even I can put asunder.' Viola is fully aware of the nature of her marriage to Wessex: 'Good morning, my lord,' she greets her groom as he collects a quick loan from her father, 'I see you are open for business – so let's to church.' *Shakespeare in Love* engages a crucial aspect of early modern marriage, the tension between the orthodox practice of arranged matches and the demands of individual choice driven by romantic love, a tension that is of course central to the play that the film's Shakespeare is writing, *Romeo and Juliet*. Elizabeth's single state, rather than a bitter sacrifice of marital bliss that leaves her hungry for false praise or entrapped in a frozen iconic image, seems instead an alternative to the restraint imposed on the film's heroine, one that allows the queen to achieve an autonomy unavailable to Viola. And while the Queen cannot break Viola's bond to Wessex, nature – in the convenient form of storm and shipwreck common in Elizabethan romance – can, providing a final image of Viola set free, 'walking away up the beach to her brave new world'.[42]

Elizabeth's dry comment that 'I know something of a woman in a man's profession, yes, by God, I do know about that' certainly suggests that her freedom is not wholly without an emotional price. But the alternative prospect of marriage to a lout like Wessex is deromanticised, and *Shakespeare in Love* thus dynamically engages the past and its practices in a way that *Elizabeth* does not, despite Shekhar Kapur's claim of a commitment to 'the emotions and essence of history' rather than to its particulars.[43] During the years when it appeared as though Elizabeth might marry, writes Christopher Hibbert, 'Her reluctance to commit herself was endlessly discussed by her councillors, to few of whom did it ever occur that a woman of such independence of spirit might actually prefer to remain single rather than submit to the loss of freedom that a marriage would entail.'[44] It's a possibility that has also been too seldom explored in the popular representation of Elizabeth, and one that *Shakespeare in Love* at least glancingly considers.

Notes

1. Robert Rosenstone, 'Reel history with missing reels', in *AHA Perspectives Online*, November 1999, American Historical Association, 21 January 2000, <www.theaha.org/perspectives/issues/1999/9911/9911fil1.cfm>, p. 2.
2. Susan Doran, 'Why did Elizabeth not marry?', in Julia Walker (ed.), *Dissing Elizabeth: negative representations of Gloriana* (Durham: Duke University Press 1998), p. 38.
3. Carole Levin, *The Heart and Stomach of a King: Elizabeth I and the politics of sex and power* (Philadelphia: University of Pennsylvania Press, 1992), p. 65.
4. Barbara Hodgdon, *The Shakespeare Trade: performances and appropriations* (Philadelphia: University of Pennsylvania Press, 1998), p. 122.
5. Lytton Strachey, *Elizabeth and Essex: a tragic history* (1928; New York: Harcourt, Brace & World, 1956), p. 24.
6. Hodgdon, *The Shakespeare Trade*, p. 124.
7. Francene Sabin, *Young Queen Elizabeth* (n.p.: Troll Associates, 1990), pp. 30, 33.
8. See Hodgdon; Renée Pigeon, 'Gloriana goes Hollywood: Elizabeth I on film, 1937–1940', in William Gentrup (ed.), *Reinventing the Middle Ages and the Renaissance: constructions of the medieval and early modern periods* (Turnout: Brepols Press, 1998), pp. 107–25.
9. Roy Strong, *Gloriana: The Portraits of Queen Elizabeth I* (London: Thames and Hudson, 1987), p. 35.
10. See Leonée Ormond, '"The spacious times of great Elizabeth": the Victorian vision of the Elizabethans', *Victorian Poetry*, 25, 3 (1987), 29–46; Strong, *Gloriana*; Strong, *Recreating the Past: British history and the Victorian painter* (London: Thames and Hudson, 1978).
11. Levin, *Heart*, p. 136.
12. Strong, *Gloriana*, p. 20.

13. Pigeon, p. 113.
14. See Hodgdon; Sharon Ouditt, 'Orlando: coming across the divide', in Deborah Cartmell and Imelda Whelehan (eds), *Adaptations: from text to screen, screen to text* (London: Routledge, 1999), pp. 146–56.
15. Virginia Woolf, *Orlando* (1928; San Diego: Harvest/HBJ, 1956), p. 22.
16. Woolf, p. 27.
17. *FQ*, II.xii.74.2–9. All references to *The Faerie Queene* are taken from the Longman edition, ed. A.C. Hamilton (London and New York: Longman, 1977).
18. Ouditt, p. 155.
19. *FQ*, II.xii.75.1–7.
20. Woolf, p. 24.
21. *FQ*, II.xii.72.1–9.
22. 'Voices', in 'The Book of Secrets', 21 January 2000, <http://www.elizabeth-the-movie.com>.
23. 'Voices'.
24. Marcia Landy, *British Genres: cinema and society, 1930–1960* (Princeton: Princeton University Press, 1996), p. 56.
25. Gemma Files, 'Like a virgin', *Rolling Eye*, 5 November, vol. 7, issue 57, 20 May 2000, <http://www.eye.net/eye/issue/issue_11.05.98/film/elizabeth.html>.
26. Richard Williams, 'Liz the Lionheart', *Guardian*, 2 October 1999, 28 May 2000, <http://www.guardianunlimited.co.uk.Archive/Article/0,4273,38,39676,000.html>.
27. Files, para. 4.
28. Lez Cooke, 'British cinema: a struggle for identity', in Clive Bloom and Gary Day (eds), *Literature and Culture in Modern Britain*, vol. 3: 1956–1999 (Harlow: Pearson Education/Longman, 2000), p. 167.
29. Claire Monk, 'The heritage film and gendered spectatorship', *Close Up: the electronic journal of British cinema*, issue 1 (1996/1997), 27 May 2000, <http://www.shu.ac.uk/services/lc/closeup/monk.htm>.
30. Strong, *Gloriana*, p. 159.
31. Carole Levin, '*Elizabeth*: Romantic film heroine or sixteenth-century queen?', *AHA Perspectives Online*, April 1999, American Historical Association, 21 January 2000, <http://www.theaha.org/perspectives/issues/1999/9904/9904FIL5.CFM>, p. 4.

32. Esther Sonnet, 'From Emma to Clueless', in Deborah Cartmell and Imelda Whelehan (eds), *Adaptations: from text to screen, screen to text* (London: Routledge, 1999), p. 57.
33. See Walker; Strong, *Gloriana*.
34. George Custen, *Bio/pics: how Hollywood constructed public history* (New Brunswick: Rutgers University Press, 1992).
35. Marcia Landy, *Cinematic Uses of the Past* (Minneapolis and London: University of Minnesota Press, 1996), p. 152.
36. 'Voices'.
37. Richard Alleva, 'The Godmother', *Commonweal*, 12 December 1998, vol. 125, issue 22, Academic Search Elite, Ebscohost, 20 May 2000.
38. Levin, *Elizabeth*, p. 4.
39. Howard Feinstein, 'The Queen and I', *Guardian*, 28 November 1998, 11 paras., 21 January 2000, <http://www.guardianunlimited.co.uk/Archive/Article/0,4273,3838618,00.html>, para. 6.
40. William Shakespeare, *Henry V*, ed. Gary Taylor (Oxford: Oxford University Press, 1984), IV.i.224–27.
41. David Walsh, '*Elizabeth* and a weakened historical sense', *World Socialist Web Site*, International Committee of the Fourth International, 21 January 2000, <http://www.wsws.org/arts/1998/dec1998/eliz-d03.shtml>.
42. Marc Norman and Tom Stoppard, *Shakespeare in Love: A Screenplay* (New York: Miramax Books/Hyperion, 1998), p. 155.
43. Williams, para. 2.
44. Christopher Hibbert, *The Virgin Queen: Elizabeth I, genius of the Golden Age* (Reading, Massachusetts: Addison-Wesley, 1991), p. 78.

3

Shakespeare in Love and the End(s) of History

Elizabeth Klett

The opening of John Madden's *Shakespeare in Love* sets up a distinct historical period: the year is 1593, the audience has entered 'the glory days of the Elizabethan theatre',[1] and is presented with the character of Will Shakespeare. Yet as the struggling young playwright repeatedly pens his name in frustration, and as that familiar penmanship lends itself to the film's titles, we are aware that something decidedly ahistorical is happening. This is confirmed when Will pitches a crumpled sheet of paper into a glossy mug embossed with 'A present from Stratford-Upon-Avon'.[2]

The film is full of such anachronisms, which include Will's punkish leather doublet, the psychoanalytic stylings of his astrologer, the boatman who tries to pitch him a script; and the waiter in a Southwark pub reciting the daily special, 'a pig's foot marinated in juniper-berry vinegar, served with a buckwheat pancake',[3] which is meant to be the sixteenth-century equivalent of *nouvelle cuisine*. The story also contains a few inaccuracies, which may or may not be intentional: Lord Wessex has tobacco plantations in Virginia before the colony was successfully founded; and, in terms of the probable composition of Shakespeare's *oeuvre*, 1593 seems a bit early for *Romeo and Juliet* and certainly too early for *Twelfth Night*.[4] Yet the filmmakers also put a lot of effort into creating an authentic period look for the film: most of the costumes are exquisitely detailed, and the settings include full-scale recreations of the Rose and Curtain theatres. The screenplay is likewise full of scrupulous research about Shakespeare's life and works. When we consider these two aspects of the film, anachronism and accuracy, it becomes evident that *Shakespeare in Love* is creating a dialectical relationship between past and present. This dialectic is predicated upon audience awareness of Shakespeare and his works, and upon the dearth of biographical data on Shakespeare's life. The result is a virtual palimpsest of texts and contexts.

Despite its anachronistic spirit, the film posits answers to two questions that have become the focus of Shakespearean scholarship and of public speculation: the authorship controversy and the 'mystery' of Shakespeare's sexuality. This paper will claim that even as *Shakespeare in Love* favours an ahistorical approach to its subject matter, it is all too ready to examine the ends of the very history it is satirising. The goal behind such a project is to reinstate Shakespeare as both authentic and as heteronormative, thereby reinvesting him with literary and social authority. The film, ultimately, re-produces the Bard as *the* dominant and popular cultural icon for our particular sociohistorical moment.

The issues of authorship and sexuality are mediated by the strategies that the film uses to market Shakespeare for a mass audience. Michael Bristol argues in *Big-Time Shakespeare* that: 'Commercial profit rather than a wish to guarantee the durable public value of Shakespeare is the motive that best accounts for the diverse enterprises of ... filmmakers.'[5] Certainly *Shakespeare in Love* was produced for commercial profit; yet I would argue that 'durable public value' ensures 'commercial profit', and vice versa. The two factors are involved in a highly symbiotic relationship; therefore, the film both produces profit and perpetuates Shakespeare's public value.

This reflection of Shakespeare as a truly popular icon is mirrored by the film's great success, and by the 'mission' of the film as stated by Madden: 'I always felt that it had the power to reach an extra-ordinarily wide demographic – everyone from groundlings to royalty.'[6] The director's choice of words here deliberately relates his film's target audience to the heterogeneous audience that was present at Shakespeare's plays;[7] therefore, he implies, the film can reach a wide variety of people because it communicates the 'true spirit' of that original theatrical experience. However, the film has been criticised for appealing too much to a certain (tiny) segment of the population: Shakespearean scholars, whose training allows them to recognise the 'in-jokes' that pepper the dialogue and situations. These include the appearance of a young and bloodthirsty John Webster, and the myriad of references to other Shakespeare plays, particularly *Hamlet* and *Antony and Cleopatra*.[8] Theatre enthusiasts also might recognise a reference to Harold Pinter's well-known complaint about audience behaviour in Will's exclamation: 'You see? The consumptives plot against me. "Will Shakespeare has a play, let us go and cough through it."'9

Much of the comedic structure of the film, in fact, is dependent upon the enactment of dramatic irony, which in turn is based on the audience's knowledge of Shakespeare's symbolic status within the culture, and also on a more concrete knowledge of his works as a whole. As a result, around the time of the film's release, articles appeared in popular newspapers and magazines advising audiences to 'brush up their Shakespeare'. Dalya Alberge's 'A Beginner's Guide to Bard Spotting' in the London *Times* is addressed to 'those who can remember only "To be or not to be" before going blank ... [Here is] a bluffer's guide to *Shakespeare in Love* that should ensure you laugh knowingly at at least *some* of the right moments.'10 This implies that there is a measure of social pressure in going to see this film: some viewers, these articles warn, may not possess the requisite cultural capital.

This gets at the crucial tension involved in *Shakespeare in Love*'s attempt at popularising Shakespeare: while it aims to divest the Bard of his intimidating iconic status and make him readily understandable to everyone, it simultaneously endorses his work as a bearer of universal values couched in the greatest poetry ever written. This flirts dangerously close to the Bardolatrous claims made by Harold Bloom in *Shakespeare: The Invention of the Human* (published, not coincidentally, just before the opening of the film). He writes: 'Shakespeare invented the human as we continue to know it ... Shakespeare ... justly imitates *essential* human nature, which is a universal and not a social phenomenon.'11 This kind of argument, while seeming to claim Shakespeare's relevance for all cultures and strata of society, only serves to make him more alienating by putting him up on a pedestal. As Bristol observes: 'The conventional value assigned to Shakespeare is connected with the belief that his works are in some way essential to the "progress of civilization." Appreciation and understanding of Shakespeare would then somehow be constitutive of membership in civilized society.'12 In other words, Shakespeare has become an elitist institution, denying 'membership' to some and welcoming others. Those who need to 'bluff' their way through *Shakespeare in Love* are therefore excluded from this rather restricted club to which Shakespearean scholars and Bardolators belong.

The film wants to have it both ways, bringing Shakespeare down to earth and setting him up on a pedestal. I would argue that it largely succeeds, due to the skilful way screenwriters Marc Norman and Tom Stoppard construct Shakespeare's character, who operates both in his historical context and out of it, like the film itself. Shakespeare is both the diegetic character who is involved in the plot that is played out onscreen, and the cultural icon whose non-diegetic life takes on all the baggage that comes with four centuries of criticism, adulation, speculation and adaptation. For the sake of clarity, throughout this chapter I will refer to the fictional creation as 'Will', as the character is called in the film. Accordingly, I will refer to the real-life author as 'Shakespeare', the icon who needs no first name in the twentieth century.

Because there are so few facts about Shakespeare's life, Norman and Stoppard invented freely, creating a Will who is as much a product of our century as of the Renaissance. As Jonathan Romney observed in a review for the *Guardian*: 'This chancer bustling round the Southwark taverns is ... kin to the wannabe screenwriters of Los Angeles or Soho today.'[13] This is the main strategy of the film's creation of the diegetic Will: he is, if not quite an ordinary Joe, certainly not a poet confined to an ivory tower with iambic pentameter flowing easily from his pen. As Joseph Fiennes, the actor who plays Will, said in an interview: 'I never felt like it was Shakespeare but a guy called Will, and he was a hustler.'[14] Similarly, Madden told the *New York Times*: 'What's special about this movie's approach, I hope, is the way it gets behind the iconic nature of the persona and paraphernalia that is Shakespeare now and deals with him in a fresh way.'[15] Shakespeare, he indicated, should be treated as a pop writer who wrote for mass audiences. More importantly, as the film's title indicates, Shakespeare should be viewed as a human being in love, something to which everyone can relate.

Audiences can also relate to Will's desperation at his inability to write; by picturing him as a hack author who wrote on commission, he becomes more accessible. Maurice Chittenden describes the 'real' Shakespeare as 'a jobbing playwright who fell into theatre because nobody would buy his poems and who used to look after the horses of the gentlefolk arriving at the theatre'.[16] This tendency to focus on Shakespeare's so-called 'humble origins', as the film does, only serves to elevate his status higher. An author of genius who emerges from the working class is a real phenomenon, more 'special' than an artist who is a member of the gentry.

Ironically, scholars have used this lack of social status as grounds for arguing that Shakespeare did not, in fact, write the plays. The authorship controversy is largely based on the assumption that 'a man of modest origins and education, who was born and died in a provincial town, could [not] have been the greatest genius in English literature'.[17] The other major factor in denying authorship to Mr Shakespeare of Stratford is due to his apparently dull and colourless life. As Joseph Sobran writes in *Alias Shakespeare*, the man (as represented by scanty biographical information) seems 'unrelated to his work. How could this nondescript man have created Falstaff and Cleopatra?'[18] Evidently, as Sobran's study demonstrates, this is a problem that has plagued Shakespeare enthusiasts for centuries.

The film also stimulated enormous interest in 'Shakespeare the man', and curiosity about the 'truth' of Shakespeare's own life, which is reflected in articles like Daniel Rosenthal's piece for the London *Times* 'Twelve Great Shakespeare Myths', which attempts to sort the fact from the fiction. Number 1 on this list is 'Shakespeare did not write any of the plays', which Rosenthal identifies as 'the big one'. He also comments: 'It may be worth bearing in mind that the first person to advocate the Earl of Oxford's claims [to authorship of the plays], in the nineteenth century, was one Thomas Looney.'[19] From Rosenthal's perspective, the authorship controversy clearly remains in the realm of mythology. The filmic creation of the Bard, however, offers a fascinating answer to this omnipresent issue. Although Will is clearly of low social status, his life is anything but dull and colourless. Moreover, his authorship is 'proven' by the clear influence of his personal life upon his art.

Will is portrayed in the film as a kind of human sponge, soaking up juicy bits of dialogue to use later in his plays. In a very early scene, as he is walking to his weekly therapy session with Dr Moth, he passes Makepeace, a street preacher, who is raging against the immorality of the theatres. He cries: 'And the Rose smells thusly rank by any name! I say a plague on both their houses! *As he passes WILL gratefully makes a mental note.*'[20] These lines, of course, turn up in *Romeo and Juliet*: the former as Juliet's 'a rose / By any other name would smell as sweet'[21]; the latter as Mercutio's dying words. Similarly, Will is shown collaborating with other authors to produce his plots. Marlowe helps him conceptualise the basic setup of *Romeo and Juliet*, which raises the issue of influence while denying Marlowe's possible authorship:

MARLOWE: Romeo is ... Italian. Always in and out of love.
WILL: Yes, that's good. Until he meets ...
MARLOWE: Ethel.

WILL: Do you think?
MARLOWE: The daughter of his enemy.
WILL (*thoughtfully*): The daughter of his enemy.
MARLOWE: His best friend is killed in a duel by Ethel's brother or something. His name is Mercutio.
WILL: Mercutio ... good name.[22]

This brief scene dramatises current scholarly views on the prevalence of collaboration in the Elizabethan theatre. Will acknowledges this influence freely after Marlowe's death, saying that '[his] touch was in my *Titus Andronicus* and my *Henry VI* was a house built on his foundations'.[23] In a similar episode, Viola de Lesseps, Will's lover, helps him to conceive the plot of *Twelfth Night*, which will be adapted from elements of their own lives. Orsino is modelled on Will, as 'the saddest wretch in the kingdom, sick with love', while the eponymous Viola undertakes 'a voyage to a new world'.[24]

Viola provides much of the inspiration for *Romeo and Juliet* as well, since it is Will's passionate relationship with her that gets his creative juices flowing again after a prolonged period of writer's block. The development of the play counterpoints their love affair, beginning with the scene in which Will crashes a party at the de Lesseps' house and falls in love with Viola at first sight. That night they play an abbreviated version of the balcony scene, in which Will prefigures the end of his tragedy: 'Oh, I am fortune's fool, I will be punished for this!'[25] Afterwards he rushes back to his garret to write Act I of his play. The camera lingers over this writing process, which is set to stirring music that lends excitement and anticipation to the scene. We are shown quick, intercutting shots of Will dipping his quill in ink, scrawling lines on the page, stripping new quills zealously, blotting ink, thinking intensely and cracking his knuckles. We see the pages of his script mounting up, and get the sense that we are watching history in the making. Just as Will is writing his play into existence, the film is inscribing the authentic Shakespeare into reality by showing him in the process of writing one of his most famous plays.

This short yet exultant scene of Will's words 'flow[ing] like a river'[26] is explicitly contrasted with the previous scenes that portray his writer's block. Before he finds inspiration in Viola, he relies on a superstitious ritual to produce his pages: '*He spins round once in a circle, rubs his hands together and spits on the floor. Then he sits down, picks up his pen, and stares in front of him.*'[27] This ritual, and his misplaced faith in Rosaline, his former mistress, are inadequate in the face of the stimulus provided by Viola. The film reinforces this both visually and aurally; in the scene where he pens Act I of the doomed *Romeo and Rosaline*, the camera uses two shots, cutting from the performance of his ritual to a low-angle close-up on his thoughtful face. The music matches this spare visual characterisation, providing a theme that is slow and contemplative. We see none of the enjoyment and orgasmic enthusiasm that is characteristic of his work on *Romeo and Juliet*.

The screenplay builds on the correlation between Will and Viola's love affair and his developing script by using a montage sequence of both in action simultaneously. In the words of Janet Maslin, film critic for the *New York Times*: 'The lovers embrace passionately while rehearsing dialogue that spills over into stage scenes, [illustrating] the bond between tempestuous love and artistic creation.'[28] This begins after they have slept together for the first time, and have subsequently rehearsed the first meeting of Romeo and Juliet onstage. As Will begins to write the balcony scene, his lines are picked up in voice-over and transport us into Viola's bedroom and onto the stage where the scene is being rehearsed. The lines between playscript, playhouse and bedchamber become so blurred that Will usurps Viola's line as Romeo:

> WILL: 'O wilt thou leave me so unsatisfied?'
> VIOLA: That's my line!
> WILL: Oh, but it is mine too![29]

The lines in his script have double meanings for them, as it becomes clear that he is writing the story of their relationship. Like Romeo and Juliet, however, Will and Viola are doomed to part tragically, which is prefigured by Viola's reading of Romeo's line at the end of the montage sequence: ' "I am afeared, / Being in night, all this is but a dream, / Too flattering-sweet to be substantial." '[30]

Will is also to return later in the composition of his play to a scene that he and Viola had played out earlier. Fellow actor Ned Alleyn suggests that he needs to add another scene, one that comes 'between marriage and death'.[31] When Viola reads it out, we realise that it is the scene after Romeo and Juliet's wedding night, in which they debate over the lark and the nightingale:

JULIET: Wilt thou be gone? It is not yet near day.
It was the nightingale, and not the lark,
That pierced the fear-full hollow of thine ear.
Nightly she sings on yon pom'granate tree.
Believe me, love, it was the nightingale.
ROMEO: It was the lark, the herald of the morn,
No nightingale.[32]

Viola also realises that he has adapted their own conversation after their first night together:

VIOLA: You would not leave me?
WILL: I must. Look – how pale the window.
VIOLA (*pulling him down*): Moonlight!
WILL: No, the morning rooster woke me.
VIOLA: It was the owl – come to bed –[33]

Aside from being a skilful re-writing of the play into more accessible (and comedic) language, the scene provides further evidence that Will is drawing on his relationship with Viola as a model for his young protagonists.

Will's tumultuous sex life with Viola also serves as 'proof' that not only was his work inspired by real events, but that Shakespeare is anything but boring, as either a writer or a lover. Viola is initially drawn to him because she loves his work: 'You [are] the highest poet of my esteem and a writer of plays that capture my heart.'[34] When they have their first sexual encounter, he initially hesitates, fearing that perhaps she is 'mistook' in him. Viola replies, 'Answer me only this: are you the author of the plays of William Shakespeare?' Will answers, 'I am.' She responds, 'Then kiss me again for I am not mistook.'[35] Will is clearly being set up as authentic and, what's more, as vibrant and passionate rather than dull and colourless.

It is important that Viola eventually falls in love with Will as a man, not simply as an author. In a scene following the revelation that it is Marlowe, and not Will, who is dead, she claims that he was 'deceived. For I never loved you till now ... I love you, Will, beyond poetry ... When I thought you dead, I did not care about all the plays that will never come, only that I would never see your face.'[36] Will, in this sense, is more than just a literary genius; he is a man worthy of love. Viola's confession reflects the film's strategy of constructing 'Shakespeare the man' to be equally as great as his work.

The visual coding of Will also counteracts the perception of Shakespeare as 'nondescript'. The filmmakers' choices in depicting him correspond heavily to Shakespeare's image as reflected in the Chandos portrait, a seventeenth-century painting by an anonymous artist that departs significantly from the famous Folio engraving by Martin Droeshout, creating a more romantic image of the Bard.[37] Sobran describes the Shakespeare of the Folio portrait as having a 'dull, pudgy face'. The Chandos image, however, is 'lean, high-domed, goateed, with penetrating eyes and an earring'. He complains that the Chandos portrait, which provides 'an arresting image of Shakespeare: intellectual but rather swashbuckling, rather like a psychoanalyst with a dash or pirate in him', does not match up with his run-of-the-mill biography.[38] However, Joseph Fiennes physically resembles the portrait in that he has a small pointed beard, an earring, and a dark, brooding demeanour. His portrayal of Will is quite swashbuckling as well, and he is certainly credited with psychoanalytic insights and piratical passions. The film is clearly drawing on the legacy of the Chandos portrait's romanticised image of Shakespeare, one which accords with his talents and with his extravagantly passionate love life as played out on screen.

Shakespeare is undeniably being made over into a sex symbol, in a way that constructs a definite answer to the 'mystery' of his sexuality. Like the authorship controversy, this has been a matter of scholarly and public speculation for some time, and the film sparked the appearance of press articles such as Jonathan Bate's piece titled 'So what is the truth about Shakespeare's own love life?' in Britain's *Daily Mail*. Bate, apparently under pressure to make the 'real' Shakespeare seem as sexy as Will, writes that: 'We are given enough hints in contemporary material to suggest young Will enjoyed a typically lascivious love life ... Shakespeare was no puritan. We know that he was not faithful to Anne Hathaway in Stratford. The passion in his work makes a strait-laced Shakespeare unlikely.'[39] In this formulation, the work produces the probable character of the man, whereas for those critics that would deny him authorship, it is the man who does not live up to the work.

The real question is, with whom was Shakespeare enjoying this 'typically lascivious love life?' Although Bate mentions the possibility of Shakespeare's bisexuality in passing, like other critics, he concentrates far more on the possible women in Shakespeare's life, rather than on his probable love, manifested in 126 of the Sonnets, for a young man. Bate speculates about the Dark Lady who inspired the later Sonnets, and on the few heterosexual stories recorded in the period about Shakespeare. These stories come up quite often in the press, and consist of the rumour that he fathered an illegitimate child, who grew up to be the poet William Davenant; and that he stole a woman from the great actor Richard Burbage, with the taunt 'William the Conqueror comes before Richard III'. Bate is of the opinion that 'the intensity of [the Sonnets] suggests a real woman with whom Shakespeare was in love', thereby conveniently endorsing the plot of the film.[40]

In order to appeal to the widest possible audience, the filmmakers had to negate Shakespeare's probable bisexuality and make him, in Chris Peachment's words, 'robustly heterosexual'.[41] The film thus participates in a long tradition of burying Shakespeare's 'shameful secret [of homosexual passion] deep within the Sonnets', by changing the addressee of the poems from male to female.[42] This is particularly the case with Sonnet 18, which begins, 'Shall I compare thee to a summer's day? / Thou art more lovely and more temperate.' Will pens the poem for Viola in the film, rather than for the fair young man it is in fact addressed to in the sonnet sequence. Although Viola is dressed as a boy when she reads the sonnet, cross-dressing consistently takes a back seat to their heterosexual love scenes. As Romney observes: 'Campery is nipped in the bud before it becomes an Elizabethan *Cage aux folles*. So much for what might have been the film's most authentically Shakespearean source for humour.'[43]

Since the sex act and the act of writing are so heavily connected in this film, we can read Will as being initiated into normative heterosexuality as the narrative progresses, so that he moves beyond both 'bad' playwrighting and possible homosexual liaisons.[44] Will himself seems painfully aware that his writer's block is intimately connected to his sexual performance; in his session with Dr Moth, he describes his problem in terms that make the connection abundantly clear: 'It's as if my quill is broken. As if the organ of the imagination has dried up. As if the proud tower of my genius has collapsed ... Nothing comes ... It is like trying to pick a lock with a wet herring.'[45] This stereotypically phallic imagery is reiterated in Burbage's infuriated challenge to Will: 'Where is that thieving hack who can't keep his pen in his own ink pot?'[46] Here, sexual one-upmanship is combined with professional one-upmanship: Burbage is angry not only because Will has given his new play to Henslowe, but because he has discovered that Will and Rosaline were having an affair.

Will's relationship with Viola ensures that both his sexual and poetic performance will be restored to him, and that he has moved beyond mediocre writing. After they make love for the first time, she expresses amazement that 'there is something better than a play'. Will concedes that her 'first try' was 'perhaps better than my first',[47] meaning that his first attempts at playwrighting were inferior. His affair with Viola also places him above the 'decadent' world of the theatre, in which he luxuriates early in the film: as he strides through Whitehall before a performance of *One Gentleman of Verona*, he fingers the wig of one boy actor and winks playfully at another. Clearly, he is comfortable in this milieu, and is primarily concerned with wheeling and dealing to get the most money out of his producers. The Will of these early scenes is a hard-headed young businessman, playing Burbage off Henslowe in his quest for the highest bidder, with no qualms about lying and cheating to get what he wants. Although he is afforded a backstage tryst with Rosaline at Whitehall, he is easily distracted from her embraces by the onstage performance and the consumptives in the audience. Until he meets Viola, he is not decisively committed to producing great art or to heterosexuality.

Viola's role-playing as Thomas Kent, the young actor who is playing Romeo in Will's production, contains the greatest possibilities for the expression of subversive sexuality, but is, in fact, used to endorse heterosexuality. This is most apparent in the scene where Viola's disguise is revealed. Viola (still dressed as Thomas) is with Will in a boat on the Thames, and asks him to tell her how he loves his lady, to whom he has been writing sonnets and sending love letters. Will launches into a Petrarchan litany of praise for her eyes, lips, voice and breasts, all the while gazing into 'Thomas's' eyes. He declares that he would defy Viola's betrothed 'for one kiss', and 'Thomas' replies by kissing him on the lips. The possible homoerotic overtones conjured by this scene are undercut by Will's response to this kiss: we get a reaction shot over Viola's shoulder that reveals his wide-eyed surprise at being kissed by a man. The screenplay emphasises that '*his words have almost unmasked her. The closeness does the rest.*'[48] If she has been 'unmasked', the riskiness of the kiss is also undercut. As she leaps out of the boat, the Boatman reveals her true identity, along with his opinion that her disguise 'wouldn't deceive a child',[49] and Will can breathe a sigh of relief. When he next sees her, she has removed her boy's wig, let down her hair, and taken off her moustache, so that they are able to kiss 'properly'. As they begin to undress each other, Viola says, 'I do not know how to undress a man', to which Will replies, 'It is strange to me, too.'[50] Will is therefore not now, nor has he ever been, homosexual.

The focus in these love scenes is on Viola undressing, particularly on the process of unwrapping her breasts. This is emphasised in this first sex scene, in a shot of Will slowly '*spin[ning] her naked*'[51] and her breasts come to signify her femininity. It is not the boy's clothes that turn Will on, but what is underneath, which has to be unwrapped and revealed. This is why the process of unbinding her breasts is given such prominence. It is also no accident that John Webster identifies Viola as a woman by saying, 'I saw her bubbies!'[52] In order to reveal her true self, he points to the physical feature that most symbolises her femininity. Although the scene in the boat is not the last time that Will kisses Viola while she is still in male garb, the audience has become privy to what is beneath 'Thomas's' clothes, and therefore any possible homoerotic edge is neatly circumvented by the revelation of her 'true' femininity.

The film also reinforces Will's heterosexuality by connecting Viola's 'real' feminine body to 'real' romantic love, which is in turn the basis for Will's 'real' genius. This theme is articulated primarily by Viola herself; early in the film, she expresses displeasure with the Elizabethan practice of using all-male casts to perform plays, exclaiming that 'stage love will never be true love while the law of the land has our heroines played by pipsqueak boys in petticoats!'[53] Her argument, ironically couched in proto-feminist rhetoric, is based in a desire for authenticity: as long as boy heroines cannot 'pass' as women, the stage will never be able to portray love accurately. *Romeo and Juliet* is judged by Queen Elizabeth to be the first play that shows 'the very truth and nature of love'.[54] The reasons for its success are twofold: Will is inspired to write the play by a 'real' woman, Viola; and the role of Juliet is played at the first performance by an actor whose 'true' gender identity is matched by her exterior shows. The audience responds accordingly, reacting to the production as though it were real: laughing, booing, cringing at the swordplay, and ultimately weeping when Romeo and Juliet kill themselves. Viola's nurse is so caught up in the performance that she responds to Juliet's rhetorical 'Where is my Romeo?' by exclaiming tearfully, 'Dead!'[55] And, of course, the audience is watching an analogue for Will and Viola's relationship, making the events that they witness 'authentic' on another level. The film's audience is encouraged to respond in kind, connecting the passion of Romeo and Juliet to the play's supposed source material: the 'real life' love between Will and Viola.

Will and Viola's romance is contained firmly within normative heterosexuality, even though the ending of the film clearly anticipates the source of Shakespeare's cross-dressed heroines in plays like *Twelfth Night* and *As You Like It*. The roles might be performed by boys dressed as women, but they will refer eternally, for Will, to his lost love: 'She will be my heroine for all time ... and her name will be ... Viola.'[56] This is perhaps the greatest ahistorical move that Norman and Stoppard make, creating the myth that Shakespeare's plays were inspired by a flesh-and-blood muse. In reality, we know for a fact that Shakespeare adapted all of his plots (including those of *Romeo and Juliet* and *Twelfth Night*) from other sources. The film blithely disregards this issue in order to focus on its re-creation of the Bard in a twentieth-century image. By creating a dialectical relationship between contemporary mythmaking and scrupulous historical accuracy, *Shakespeare in Love* circumvents the need to solve the unsolvable mystery of the 'real' Shakespeare, and instead creates a persona that will appeal to the widest possible audience. Authentic, heterosexual, passionate, sexy, and funny, Will is reborn as the ultimate culturally accessible icon, proving that he is not just for an age, but for our time.

Notes

1. Marc Norman and Tom Stoppard, *Shakespeare in Love: a screenplay* (New York: Hyperion, 1998), p. 1.
2. Ibid., p. 5.
3. Ibid., p. 27.
4. The Oxford Shakespeare dates *Romeo and Juliet* as written in either 1594 or 1595; *Twelfth Night* is dated around 1601.
5. Michael D. Bristol, *Big-Time Shakespeare* (London and New York: Routledge, 1996), p. x.
6. Quoted in Jeff Dawson, 'In love with Will', *Daily Telegraph* (16 January 1999), p. A5.
7. For a thorough discussion of the audiences who attended the theatre during Shakespeare's time, see Andrew Gurr, *The Shakespearean Stage, 1574–1642* (Cambridge: Cambridge University Press, 1980), pp. 195–215.
8. These references include, but are not limited to, the following: Will's evasive reply to Henslowe, 'Doubt that the stars are fire,

doubt that the sun doth move,' (p. 6) is from Hamlet's letter to Ophelia (II.ii.116–17). In therapy with Dr Moth, who takes his name from the pageboy in *Love's Labour's Lost* (p. 9), Will anticipates Hamlet's 'Words, words, words' (II.ii.195). Viola's diatribe against 'pipsqueak boys in petticoats' (p. 20) who are unable to impersonate women accurately, is analogous to Cleopatra's certainty that she will 'see / Some squeaking Cleopatra boy my greatness' (V.ii.218–19). Will orders 'Give me to drink mandragora' (p. 28) in a pub, as in *Antony and Cleopatra* (I.v.3). His aborted first-day speech to his actors recalls Peter Quince's similar speech in *A Midsummer Night's Dream* (I.ii). He describes his love for Viola as 'sickness and its cure together' (p. 65), anticipating Sonnet 147, which begins, 'My love is as a fever, longing still / for that which longer nurseth the disease.' Will's ghost-like appearance to Wessex in the church (p. 110) plays like Macbeth's half-crazed apprehension of Banquo's ghost (III.iv). His conversation with Viola in the following scene (pp. 111–13) is drawn from Hamlet's encounter with Ophelia (III.i). In the same scene, 'it needed no wife come from Stratford to tell you that' (p. 112) paraphrases Horatio's 'There needs no ghost, my lord, come from the grave / To tell us this' (I.v.129–30). The references to *Antony and Cleopatra* are rounded out by Will's parting words to Viola: 'You will never age for me, nor fade, nor die' (p. 153), which anticipate Enobarbus's lines about Cleopatra: 'Age cannot wither her, nor custom stale / Her infinite variety' (II.ii.241–2).

 9. Norman and Stoppard, *Shakespeare in Love*, p. 17.
10. Dalya Alberge, 'A beginner's guide to Bard-spotting', *The Times* (23 January 1999), p. 21.
11. Harold Bloom, *Shakespeare: the Invention of the human* (New York: Riverhead Books, 1998), pp. 2–3.
12. Bristol, *Big-Time Shakespeare*, p. 8.
13. Jonathan Romney, 'A Bard day's night', *Guardian* (29 January 1999), p. 8.
14. Quoted in Martyn Palmer, 'The player', *The Times*, Magazine (9 January 1999), p. 20.
15. Quoted in Bernard Weinraub, 'Stratfordians', *New York Times* (11 December 1998), p. E16.
16. Maurice Chittenden, 'Wherefore art thou, Will?', *Sunday Times* (24 January 1999), p. 13. Shakespeare's job as a valet is one of

those legends that has never been proven. Chittenden is engaged in his own brand of mythmaking here.

17. Joseph Sobran, *Alias Shakespeare: solving the greatest literary mystery of all time* (New York: The Free Press, 1997), p. 1.
18. Ibid., p. 2.
19. Daniel Rosenthal, 'Twelve great Shakespeare myths', *The Times* (27 January 1999), p. 34. The other eleven myths are: '1) Shakespeare had collaborators on several plays, 2) Shakespeare wrote some of the best parts for himself, 3) Shakespeare was a Catholic, 4) Shakespeare was a soldier, 5) Shakespeare was a teacher, 6) Shakespeare was bisexual, 7) Shakespeare was an adulterer, 8) Shakespeare had a love-child, 9) Shakespeare was a poacher, 10) Shakespeare was a teenage animal-rights activist, 11) The Bard died from booze.' Several of these myths figure both in *Shakespeare in Love* and in the press surrounding the film.
20. Norman and Stoppard, *Shakespeare in Love*, pp. 8–9. Quotations in italics are stage directions in the published script.
21. William Shakespeare, *Romeo and Juliet*, in Stanley Wells and Gary Taylor (eds), *The Complete Works* (Oxford: Clarendon Press, 1988), II.i.85–6.
22. Norman and Stoppard, *Shakespeare in Love*, p. 30.
23. Ibid., p. 111.
24. Ibid., pp. 151–2.
25. Ibid., p. 46.
26. This is Dr Moth's promise to Will, p. 12.
27. Ibid., p. 20.
28. Janet Maslin, 'Shakespeare saw a therapist?', *New York Times* (11 December 1998), p. E16.
29. Norman and Stoppard, *Shakespeare in Love*, p. 82.
30. Ibid., p. 84.
31. Ibid., p. 115.
32. Shakespeare, *Romeo and Juliet*, III.V.1–7.
33. Norman and Stoppard, *Shakespeare in Love*, p. 71.
34. Ibid., p. 46.
35. Ibid., p. 68.
36. Ibid., p. 112.
37. *O Sweet Mr Shakespeare, I'll Have His Picture: the changing image of Shakespeare's person, 1600–1800* (London: National Portrait Gallery, 1964), p. 12.
38. Sobran, *Alias Shakespeare*, p. 11.

39. Jonathan Bate, 'So what is the truth about Shakespeare's own love life?', *Daily Mail* (22 January 1999), p. 11. Note the commingling of names here: Bate uses both 'Will' and 'Shakespeare' to refer to the historical subject, which manifests the clear influence of the film upon his theories.

40. Ibid. The Davenant story is also referenced by Rosenthal in his piece on Shakespearean mythology. The slight against Burbage is reiterated in the film when Burbage discovers that Will has been seeing his mistress Rosaline on the side.

41. Chris Peachment, 'A ruff guide to the amorous Bard', *Mail on Sunday* (31 January 1999), p. 34.

42. Margreta de Grazia, 'The scandal of Shakespeare's sonnets', *Shakespeare Survey*, 46 (1994), p. 36.

43. Romney, 'A Bard day's night', p. 8.

44. I am grateful to Carol Thomas Neely for suggesting this idea to me.

45. Norman and Stoppard, *Shakespeare in Love*, pp. 10–11.

46. Ibid., p. 99.

47. Ibid., p. 70. Interestingly, Will's reply is not in the film, although it appears in the screenplay. Why it was cut is anyone's guess; perhaps the filmmakers did not want to admit that Shakespeare's early attempts at playwrighting were 'bad'.

48. Ibid., p. 67.

49. Ibid.

50. Ibid., pp. 68–9.

51. Ibid., p. 69.

52. Ibid., p. 121.

53. Ibid., p. 20.

54. Ibid., p. 95.

55. Ibid., pp. 144–5.

56. Ibid., pp. 154–5.

4

Reflections on Sex, Shakespeare and Nostalgia in Trevor Nunn's *Twelfth Night*

Maria F. Magro and Mark Douglas

The date of 23 April 2000 was celebrated as usual as St George's Day and the anniversary of Shakespeare's birth in 1564. It was also the feast of Easter in the ecclesiastical calendar. BBC Radio 3 marked this millennial intersection of Christianity, nationality and sanctioned culture by dedicating the day's programming to Shakespeare. One week later, Carol Vorderman, British television's reigning popular intellectual, failed to identify Sir Toby Belch as the comic knight in *Twelfth Night* when she appeared on the May Day celebrity edition of ITV's top-rating gameshow *Who Wants to be a Millionaire?* Vorderman's subsequent avowal that the work of Shakespeare is 'dull as ditchwater' was widely quoted in the media. Now, it is neither the intention of this chapter to adjudicate between these competing evaluations of the contemporary status and social value of Shakespeare's work nor to engage in questions about the complex aesthetic codes, educational capital and cultural competencies at stake in the making of such judgements. Rather, we aim to examine Trevor Nunn's recent cinematic treatment of Shakespeare's *Twelfth Night* (1996), which makes claim to the contemporary representation of sexuality despite its period setting and framing. Our concerns here are two-fold. First, we will figure this conservative representation of Shakespeare in the context of the contemporary ascendancy of the costume drama and the nostalgic mood of 1990s television and cinema. Secondly, we seek to establish and contextualise what we argue are politically reactionary *naturalisations* of white heterosexuality in Nunn's film by placing it within a *fin de siècle* cultural milieu which insistently promulgates a sexual ideology in which white, heterosexual and, ultimately, monogamous sex is figured as the constitutive model for sexual behaviour and subjectivity.

The current vogue for costume drama genre in television and cinema was initiated by the commercial successes of Merchant–Ivory's sanitised and romanticised reinventions of the past, beginning with the adaptation of E.M. Forster's *A Room with a View* (1985). In fact, the latter was released in the wake of David Lean's orientalist epic *A Passage to India* (1984). These soft-focus texts and their proliferating progeny offer preferred strategies of historical understanding by encoding history, colonialism and the aesthetics of English class stratification within seductive codes of linear narrativity, melodrama and visual spectacle. The latter codes obviate historical contradictions, cultural ruptures and social tensions (those moments in which the explanatory power of history as linear and progressive breaks down) and in their place insert the totalising myth of heterosexual romantic love, set, usually, within an exotic, heritage or pastoral *mise-en-scène*. The success of these films, we suggest, lies not only in their spectacular appeal (lavish costumes, scenery and locations) but also in the fact that they give the armchair historian facile, easy-to-employ decoding strategies for making sense of the historical process. In this respect Nunn's decision to set his production of *Twelfth Night* in 'West Barbary', the wild and romantic landscape of Cornwall (Lanhydrock, Prideaux Place, St Michael's Mount), functions to idealise and abstract the historical context of the film, creating a dispersed sense of nostalgia for the romantic, lyrical countryside. In the same manner the 'Globe–heritage' representation of early modern London in John Madden's *Shakespeare in Love* (1998) engages the nostalgic myth of pre-industrial metropolitan life and theatrical community.[1]

The analysis of *Twelfth Night* in terms of its channelling of erotic desire into heteronormative narration does not in itself represent a particularly new trend in cultural criticism (Butler, Rubin, Sedgwick). What is interesting about this pre-millennial film, however, is the manner in which it seeks to establish a sexual mythology within the cultural framework of late Victorian England. We are interested in both why and how at this particular historical conjunction the Shakespearean texts and author-function are used as cultural masterpieces and paternal author(ity) for legitimating and buttressing what are clearly late twentieth-century discourses on sex. What is of particular interest here is the dramatic mobilisation of *Twelfth Night*, arguably Shakespeare's most provocative text in its representation of ambivalent sexual object-choice and culturally shaped discourses of desire, in creating a nostalgic myth of romantic, courtly love for both popular and middle-brow consumption. In Nunn's cinematic revisioning, moments of gender and sexual ambiguity involving mis-recognition and misrepresentation are ultimately used to reaffirm established, normative heterosexuality, rather than asserting the existence and positive cultural value of diverse and multiple sexualities.

The alliance between the Shakespeare sign and narratives of romantic heterosexuality strikes us as a particularly uneasy one. Craig Dionne has pointed out how in the context of North American popular culture the Shakespeare sign is configured as something outside or 'in excess of heterosexuality'.[2] Likewise, the cultural work that Shakespeare and his textual production perform in *Twelfth Night*, while nostalgically presenting a cultural system purged of non-straight sexualities, overflows its own signifying boundaries. There is a representational surplus in this film and other contemporary rep-resentations of Shakespeare and his texts that allows for the decon-struction of their ostensibly homophobic meaning. In other words, the de-queering of Shakespeare suggests that a queer Shakespeare may be lurking uneasily beneath the surface.

Film, Nostalgia and Shakespeare

The proliferation of period and costume drama genres in British and American cinema and television during the 1980s and 1990s is symptomatic of an Anglo-American cultural obsession with the past, reflected too in the rise in the popularity of historical theme parks ranging from Greenfield Village in Dearborn, Michigan, to the web of country houses and gardens making up the British heritage industry. The connections here are mutually reinforcing. Imelda Whelehan has noted, for example, that 'Lyme Hall in Cheshire, used to represent Pemberley in the 1995 adaptation of *Pride and Prejudice*, is a National Trust property accustomed to around 800 visitors a week late in the season; yet, in the autumn of 1995, 5500 visitors arrived during the final two days of opening'.[3] This postmodern commodification of the past signifies a cultural immersion in a nostalgia so thick and impenetrable that, as Frederic Jameson has observed, 'we are unable today to focus on our own present, as though we have become incapable of achieving aesthetic represen-tations of our current experience'.[4] Jameson ascribes this mode of nostalgia to films that not only directly represent the past but also to those films like *Star Wars* that convey the past metonymically.

That is, while *Star Wars* is ostensibly a narrative of futuristic inter-galactic heroes and villains, its central tropes culturally enact a deep American yearning to return to the innocence of the 1950s 'Saturday afternoon serial of the Buck Rogers type',[5] a period which for white American cinema and television audiences iconically signifies a moment of pre-lapsarian wholesomeness. Here the nostalgic motive in fact encodes in symbolic forms the political unconscious of a white supremacist culture, the unspeakable desire to return to the Eisenhower era, a time prior to mass mobilisations in the name of civil rights against racist and sexist power hierarchies.

Germane to this point is Lynn Spigel's research into women's popular memory, 1950s sitcom reruns and nostalgia shows on North American network and cable television. Spigel found that while some of the research participants acknowledged 'these television images were more exclusive to the white middle class than repre-sentative of all women',[6] this acknowledgment by no means precluded 'backlash discourses' pitting 'femininity against feminism' and the construction of the 1950s by way of 'nostalgic longing for the "good old days" when girls were girls and boys made money'.[7] It is also worth noting here that Trevor Nunn's decision to place his production of *Twelfth Night* in the late Victorian era stemmed from a desire to have the film 'set at a time when, in their silhouette, men were clearly men – no frills and lace – and when conversely women were expected to be very cosmetic, frail and delicate creatures, to be protected from the harsher realities'.[8]

The dialectical logic of Jameson's analysis of film and nostalgia invites possible reconfigurations or reversals of the terms of that analysis. Accordingly if films about the future can convey the past metonymically, then films set in the past can be decoded as metonymic representations of present cultural and political debates. In this context, the political unconscious of the costume drama provides a framework for understanding how the genre functions as a 'safe' signifying space for articulating ideas that may not be acceptably aired in contemporary cinema. In other words, the historical milieu of these productions provides an alibi for the industry that produces them; a director can always argue that she is not providing a forum for regressive politics, rather, 'that's just the way it was back then'. Such a move brings to the fore the issue of history and its relationship to contemporary culture. The question then shifts from why period or costume dramas are so popular with contemporary audiences to how history functions as a sign in cinema and in popular memory. Following Spigel we understand popular memory as those constructions of the past 'enmeshed in knowledge circulated by dominant social institutions',[9] particularly by television and cinema. What exactly is the costume drama made to speak that cannot be spoken in films which directly represent contemporary culture? Despite their patently conservative stance *vis-à-vis* cultural discourses of sexuality, do these films offer the possibility for oppositional readings? And, more to the point of this chapter, how and why are Shakespeare's name and works invoked in postmodern costume dramas? Does Shakespeare as author-function have a stable signifying meaning?[10]

As we noted above, the current ubiquity of costume drama in television and cinema was inaugurated by the commercial success and critical acclaim of films such as *A Room With a View* (1985), *Howards End* (1992) and *The Remains of the Day* (1993), all from the production team of Ismail Merchant and James Ivory. Merchant–Ivory films demonstrated to audiences, the film industry and critics alike that the costume drama was not an obsolescent genre doomed to commercial morbidity. Quite the contrary, as Lynda E. Boose and Richard Burt remark:

> Up until the very recent Jane Austen fueled and Merchant–Ivory underwritten revival of period film anything considered 'classical' had become equated with a kind of artsy-fartsy cultural elitism that was bound not to make money and was something thus left to the independent film producer aiming at the art houses or the Sundance film festival.[11]

Exotic locales, lavish and 'authentic' period costumes and the omnipresent romantic diegesis have an appeal for both middlebrow and popular audiences trained in the conventions of the Hollywood style. History in these films invites audience identification with residual modes of gentility and the melodramatic entanglements of love: the otherness of the past is glossed over and the temporal and cultural distance signified by period costumes and historical locations are foreshortened by familiar narrative discourses, stable actors, intertextual references and the romantic spectacle of heterosexual melodrama.

An exemplary text in respect of this cinematic elision of history is Anthony Minghella's blockbuster adaptation of Michael Ondaatje's *The English Patient* (1996). In the first instance, John Seale's epic desert photography combines with the poignant romance of the plot to mystify the story's colonial setting. Secondly, the narrative of political betrayal – Ralph Fiennes's role as Nazi collaborator – is intersected by the melodramatic narrative of romantic treachery and duplicity and appears to offer a dubious exit from history. In *The English Patient*, then, the complexity and contradictions of history are ironed out; social relations are simplified to be displaced onto the romance of the white, heterosexual main characters. Audiences can leave the cinema (or the sofa) assured, in the slogan of the middlebrow North American Arts & Entertainment cable channel, that this was 'time well spent'. Here they have absorbed a bit of history, been entertained and avoided the sort of ethical complacency encouraged by, say, going to see a shock genre piece like *Scream 3*.

The catalogue of film titles listed above suggests that the nineteenth century remains a popular historical period for the costume drama. Notably, Branagh's *Hamlet*, Hoffman's *A Midsummer's Night Dream* and Nunn's *Twelfth Night* all eschew a Renaissance backdrop for nineteenth- or turn-of-the-century settings.[12] Citing Giddings *et al.*, Imelda Whelehan suggests that recycling of nineteenth-century settings in the historical drama is due, in part, to their historical accessibility; the nineteenth century is, after all, relatively recent history.[13] Whelehan further observes that the craving for images of the nineteenth century on big and small screens 'are all symptomatic of the condition of the national psyche which is shedding layers of modernity and reverting to its own past tones under the stress of contemporary economic, political and social crisis'.[14] Similarly, Spigel found in her research into women's popular memory and reruns of 1950s sitcoms widespread 'nostalgia for a better past'[15] represented in the worlds of *Leave it to Beaver* and the 1950s pastiche *Happy Days*.

However, what do we make of recent films dealing with either the Renaissance or the Shakespeare author-function and their critical and commercial popularity? Nunn's *Twelfth Night*, *Elizabeth* (Shekhar Kapur, 1998) and *Shakespeare in Love* bear witness to the increasing popularity of the Renaissance and Shakespeare as tropes amenable to the commercially lucrative codes of the costume drama; *Shakespeare in Love* was nominated for an impressive thirteen Academy Awards and won seven, including Best Picture, Best Actress and Best Original Screenplay, while *Elizabeth* was nominated for Best Picture and Best Actress. All of this at a time when pundits are bemoaning the decline of Shakespeare in the classroom and the 'dumbing down' of university and college English Literature curriculum,[16] and when the G2 section of the *Guardian* featured a cover picture of the Bard overlaid by a multiple-choice question text, *à la Who Wants to Be a Millionaire?* 'Question: "Who is this Very Famous Man?" Possible answers: A: William Shakespeare, B: William the Conquerer, C: William Hague, D: Who Cares?'[17]

Unlike the nineteenth century, neither the Renaissance nor Shakespeare has the advantage of historical proximity. Indeed, for the majority of contemporary viewers Elizabethan England must seem oddly foreign, another world. A symptomatic reading of nostalgia in film and television productions in which representations of Elizabethan England or the Bardic voice signal crises in the national psyche is one mode of understanding the putative nostalgia these texts evince. Another, complementary mode, we suggest, is to interrogate the meaning(s) these films create through their formal techniques and diegesis and ask why those meanings were rendered in the format of the costume drama. In other words, what kind of alibis do the costume drama and Shakespeare as legitimating author-function provide? What are adaptations of a text like *Twelfth Night* saying about *contemporary* sex and gender issues? Could the same meaning be created in an adaptation of the play that had a contemporary setting? And finally, what are the relationships between questions of nostalgia, authenticity and fidelity in adaptations of Shakespearean texts?

Gender Trouble in Illyria: Trevor Nunn's *Twelfth Night*

Trevor Nunn's adaptation of *Twelfth Night* sees itself as offering a sophisticated and even postmodern interpretation of Shakespeare's complex rendering of Renaissance gender confusion. The website for the film's video release boldly proclaims that '[b]efore Priscilla crossed the desert, Wong Foo met Julie Newmar, and the Birdcage was unlocked, there was *Twelfth Night*'.[18] Through the invocation of contemporary films that treat matters such as cross-dressing, homosexuality and gender misrecognition the website suggests that the Renaissance text of *Twelfth Night* historically precedes them. Nunn's adaptation of *Twelfth Night*, the publicity proposes, is both modern *and* true to the integral meaning of Shakespeare's text. For Nunn *Twelfth Night* 'is an examination of gender; Shakespeare is fascinated with what is attractive about the woman in man and the man in woman. "Gender-bending" we call it these days.'[19] Presumably the gender and sexual issues in the primary text are retained in this film version. According to this logic Nunn's film satisfies the opposing demands of authenticity and postmodern sophistication without sacrificing either. Nunn's valorisation of authenticity is evinced even in the casting of the film. Accordingly, Telluride's corporate publicity for the film announces the superiority of British theatre-trained actors and their mannered speech over Hollywood stars who are unable to 'speak Shakespeare's lines': 'the film succeeds in part due to Nunn's decision to ignore the box-office lure of Hollywood stars, and to cast all the parts with outstanding British actors who can actually speak Shakespeare's lines with proper cadence and clarity'.[20] If the casting decisions signify Nunn's fidelity to the aural style of British Shakespearean performance, his alteration of dialogue, scenes and historical setting of the primary text positions him as an experimental director who is willing to take liberties with the source material.

Following from this assumption, the publicity material and *Twelfth Night* itself draw on contemporary understandings of gender and non-straight sexualities, suggesting that the Renaissance text understands gender and sexuality in a manner similar to the late twentieth century. The historical distance between Shakespeare's text (*c.* 1601) and contemporary models of gender and sexuality is telescoped to the point where difference is put under erasure. Drawing on the familiar humanist assumption that human nature is essentially the same across historical epochs and cultural milieus, both publicity material and film represent sexuality as fundamentally unvarying. This counter-factual assumption projects the same universal sexual scheme across widely divergent cultural contexts in the name of the transhistorical and transcultural Bard. Under the auspices of this false universality, three drag queens crossing the Australian outback and confronting often violent homophobia is equivalent to a pastoral romp in the fictional land of Illyria. Shakespeare is the universal signifier who does the cultural work of aestheticising what are political issues. It is precisely because of the social legitimacy of Shakespeare as a sign of high culture that adjacent universalising tropes come into play.

Contrary to the ahistorical construction of sexuality and gender posited above, the aligning of sexuality and gendered subjectivity with identity is a nineteenth-century phenomenon. In modern

Western culture sex has had an increasingly privileged relationship to truth about the self. In the first volume of *The History of Sexuality,* Michel Foucault argues that the Christian tradition of sexual confession gradually evolved into a *scienta sexualis*:

> nearly one hundred and fifty years have gone into the making of a complex machinery for producing true discourses on sex: a deployment that spans a wide segment of history in that it connects the ancient injunction of confession to clinical listening methods. It is this deployment that enables something called 'sexuality' to embody the truth of sexuality and its pleasures.[21]

Sex, then, has since the nineteenth century been framed as an epistemological issue from which two processes emerge: 'we demand that sex speak the truth ... and we demand that it tell us our truth, or rather, the deeply buried truth of that truth about ourselves which we think we possess in our deeply buried consciousness'.[22] It is significant, then, that Nunn's *Twelfth Night* poses problems of sex and gender as problems of truth. Here the problem of truth is metonymically played out through the truth of Viola's identity as a woman and the socially sanctioned couplings that resolve the gender confusion.[23]

The opening scene of Nunn's *Twelfth Night* is suggestive of the gender confusion touted in the website publicity material. Dressed as veiled harem girls, the identical twins Viola (Imogen Stubbs) and Sebastian (Steven Macintosh) are shown entertaining the other guests on a ship with the musical number 'O mistress mine'. As they sing, the sound of a baritone male voice (Sebastian's) gives the lie to the illusion that both performers are female soprano or mezzo-soprano singers. This auditory effect 'is actually achieved by alternately overdubbing two female voices and one male voice'.[24] However, since both performers are veiled and heavily made-up it is impossible at the visual level to ascertain which harem girl is really a man. The humour of the scene derives from a regressive striptease in which Sebastian turns to Viola and removes her veil. Viola, however, is wearing a moustache and so appears at first to be the female impersonator. To the delight of the other passengers, Sebastian tears off Viola's moustache, exposing her impersonation of a man impersonating a woman. Viola then removes Sebastian's veil, revealing another moustachioed harem girl. Just as Viola prepares to expose the 'true' impersonator by attempting to remove Sebastian's (real) moustache, the ship founders.

As Richard Burt has pointed out, this scene 'raises the possibility of an infinite regress of false revelations in which any gender marker always has to be put in quotation marks as a performative signifier'.[25] The stripping away of accretive layers of gender signifiers (voice, veil, moustache) illustrates Judith Butler's point that gender is a performance whose signifying gestures posit an originary or authentic sexual identity. 'Gender is the repeated stylisation of the body, a set of repeated acts within a highly rigid regulatory frame that congeal over time to produce the appearance of substance, of a natural sort of being.'[26]

The drag sequence in the opening scene raises the prospect that the film will perform a critique of the fixity of sexual identity and the 'naturalness' of gender. However, this expectation is soon undermined by two contrary performative elements. At the same time that the film uses a technological apparatus to undercut the assumption that voice is an essentially gendered characteristic, it invokes the sovereign author-function, the anchoring voice of the patriarchal Bard-as-storyteller. Speaking in 'pseudo-Elizabethan verse',[27] the male voiceover of the prologue begins: 'I'll tell thee a tale. Now list to me ...' As the opening credits appear on the screen the voiceover is interwoven with the film's thematic music – the nostalgic 'The Rain It Raineth Every Day'. The male voiceover inter-polates the drag scene and subsequent shipwreck for the film audience. The authoritative voice of the omniscient narrator, Shakespeare as storyteller, guides the spectator's vision through the title sequence by steering our attention away from the gender-bending of the preceding drag sequence to the 'real' genders of the twins and the high drama of the shipwreck. Absurdly, though the ship is in imminent danger of sinking, Sebastian still has time to wipe off his make-up and don masculine attire – a naval officer's uniform – while Viola hurriedly removes her long black wig to reveal 'natural' long blond hair. The suggestion here is crucial to the logic of the narrative: the prologue must establish the authentic genders of the twins before the film proper can begin.

The male voiceover also provides a distraction from the second element of the scene that we wish to foreground – the Antonio character. In many readings of the play, Antonio is singled out as a gay character,[28] the Antonio/Sebastian frustrated love story serving as a parallel to the other 'false' romances in the narrative based on gender misrecognition (Cesario/Olivia), obsessive desire (Orsino/Olivia), social promotion (Malvolio/Olivia) and comic courting (Andrew Aguecheek/Olivia). Excluded from the heterosexual economy and potential procreative plenitude of the play's final scene, Antonio's desire for Sebastian is frequently interpreted as having no place in the traditional comedic finale, the pairing-off of the principal characters. The text of the play, however, is vague concerning Antonio's actions, demeanour and physical positioning in this final scene, offering no stage direction. Taking into consideration the play's silence on this matter, the way in which a production deals with the Antonio character can provide an index to how that production envisages the sexual meaning and possibilities of the narrative.

The opening sequence of Nunn's film is organised by a shot/reverse-shot camera movement that links the performing twins by a long-shot to medium close-up of Antonio (Nicholas Farrell). This establishes an (homo)erotic triangulation which the film will eventually disavow. As the ship breaks upon the rocks, Viola is thrown overboard. While Antonio attempts to hold him back, Sebastian desperately throws himself into the water to save his sister. The twins are temporarily reunited under water in a moment of amniotic oneness, only to be separated by a strong current that 'divides what naught had ever kept apart'. Though the voiceover insists that the strong currents and sinking boat are responsible for severing Viola and Sebastian, the visual logic and dramatic action of the scene position Antonio as the dividing element between the twins. Antonio tries to stop Sebastian from jumping in after Viola and, at the moment the twins are separated, he is preparing to jump into the water to save Sebastian (Viola has already been rescued by the captain). This complex visual diegesis combines with the matrimonial parlance of the voiceover – 'what naught had ever kept apart' – to suggest that Antonio is a dramatic bar between the twins and symbolically disruptive of stable heterosexual relations.

The climatic pairing-off sequence in Nunn's *Twelfth Night* restores the 'natural perspective' (V.i.217)[29] by which all the plot's misunderstandings and misrecognitions are resolved into authentic genders and desire is demonstrated to be essentially heterosexual. In this heteronormative context, as Olivia (Helena Bonham Carter) and Sebastian and Viola and Orsino (Toby Stephens) pair off happily, Antonio looks on with a slightly poignant but accepting smile, an attitude of resigned tolerance in the face of the inevitable romantic closure of the narrative. Along with Feste (Ben Kingsley), Sir Andrew Aguecheek (Richard E. Grant) and Malvolio (Nigel Hawthorne), Antonio is shown leaving Olivia's house to clear the way for the finale in which the couples, dressed according to their appropriate genders, perform a nuptial country dance. This pairing-off scene echoes the drag scene at the beginning of the film by having Sebastian peel away Viola-Cesario's moustache to reveal the 'real' Viola underneath. The pairing-off scene, however, enacts a closure that is only partially achieved by the interruption of the shipwreck in the early drag scene. In fact, the entire narrative structure of the film pushes toward the ultimate closing down of radical possibilities for gender identification and sexual identity.

The audience is given privileged knowledge about Viola's transformation into the male courtier Cesario. After the shipwreck, Viola finds herself on the foreign and hostile shores of Illyria and, believing her brother to have been drowned, strategically dons masculine attire and presents herself at the all-male court of the Count Orsino. With the aid of the captain who saved her, Viola transforms herself into a dashing if slightly fey young man. Her spectacular transformation involves the casting away of her feminine garments (dress, corset, shoes, jewellery), cutting her hair, binding her breasts, stuffing her trousers with a rag, and learning to walk and talk like a male courtier. Her masquerade works so well that she is accepted into Orsino's court and becomes Olivia's object of desire.

It is significant that, as Richard Burt argues, there is never any question of the articulation of lesbian desire in Nunn's *Twelfth Night*. Olivia's attraction to Cesario and Cesario's resultant consternation is played 'strictly for laughs'.[30] During the scene in which Olivia declares her love for Cesario, the camera lingers on Cesario's discomfiture and since we are in on the trick of her disguise we are forced to identify with Cesario's comical distress. The foreclosure on lesbian representation and desire in Nunn's *Twelfth Night* (like the 'gender-bending' twentieth-century films with which it is favourably compared) and exclusive concern with homoerotic possibilities between men is ultimately symptomatic of its sexual conservatism. That is, unlike *Priscilla Queen of the Desert*, *Twelfth Night* finally attempts to contain the very potential for same-sex desire it has explored.

The moment of negation of same-sex desire occurs in a sequence in which Cesario and Orsino are being serenaded by a guitar-playing Feste. Notably, the film comes teasingly close to allowing for same-sex desire on the part of Orsino. As Feste sings a romantic tune Cesario and Orsino lean close together and Cesario slowly tilts up his head to kiss Orsino. At the moment their lips are on the point of touching, Feste (who the film suggests is aware that Cesario is a woman; he has seen her emerge from a cave following the shipwreck and will return her cast-off necklace in the revelation scene) ends the song and Cesario and Orsino abruptly separate. Feste's reaction is one of feigned unawareness. This scene repeats the erotic triangle set-up at the beginning of the film between Sebastian, Viola and Antonio. This triangulation, however, sets the heterosexual structure of the narrative to rights. Rather than Antonio's intervening and destabilising homoerotic gaze, here the voyeuristic gaze of Feste brings Orsino and Cesario together. It is significant that, like the audience, Feste is in on the joke and hence his gaze functions to bring about the heterosexual resolution of the film. Notably, in the shot/reverse-shot movement that structures this scene, the camera's point of view is both that of Feste and an omniscient observer. As he plays the guitar, Feste is seated to the left of and below Cesario and Orsino. The camera is initially positioned over Feste's left shoulder. We see what he sees: the developing intimacy between Orsino and Cesario. However, as the scene unfolds, the camera observes Cesario and Orsino in profile, a point of view that Feste clearly cannot possess. The viewer is thereby also drawn into the erotic triangulation as voyeur as well. Knowing what Feste appears to know, that Cesario is a woman, the audience can safely indulge in some homoerotic titillation without guilt.[31] Importantly, it is the male gaze (Feste's and the camera's) that orchestrates the heterosexual rapprochement of the film. In brief, not only does Nunn's *Twelfth Night* attempt to put homosexuality under erasure but it also legitimates the authority and potency of the male gaze.

What is particularly interesting here is that the terms of this legitimisation of the male gaze are predicated upon Feste's nonparticipation in the heterosexual discourse of romance. That is, the voyeuristic economy depends expressly upon Feste's diegetic role as narrator; Feste observes and orchestrates the erotic triangulation, functioning as narrative copula but never as the subject or object of desire. This voyeuristic quality, the structures of observation, vision and narration, are in fact the characteristics ascribed by Viola to the professional fool:

> This fellow's wise enough to play the fool;
> And, to do that well, craves a kind of wit:
> He must *observe* their mood on whom he jests,
> The quality of the persons, and the time;
> And, like the haggard, check at every feather
> That comes before his *eye*. This is a practice
> As full of labour as a wise man's art.
> (III.i. 60–66, emphasis added)

Viola's soliloquy, of course, is also a metacommentary on the attributes of the professional playwright. At several points in Nunn's *Twelfth Night* there is the suggestion that Feste occupies the position of the Shakespeare author-function. The film's theme song 'The Rain It Raineth Every Day' is a framing vehicle whereby the author-function is articulated through Feste as performer. To reiterate, the title sequence establishes and connects an authorial voice with the musical theme while the closing shots link Feste's rendition of the theme song with the insistent heteronormativity of the dance finale. Similarly, Richard Burt has noted that the voyeuristic character of the Shakespeare persona is a recurrent trope in pornographic treatments of Shakespearean texts. Here he is present only to oversee but never to participate in the sexual economy. This nonproductive, one might even say queer sexuality, can be opposed to the Romantic and Freudian rendition of Will's erotic persona in Madden's *Shakespeare in Love*. In this volume, Elizabeth Klett rightly observes that Will's authorial productivity is represented in 'stereotypically phallic imagery':

> Will himself seems painfully aware that his writer's block is intimately connected to his sexual performance; in his session with Dr Moth, he describes his problem in terms that make the connection abundantly clear: 'It's as if my quill is broken. As if the organ of the imagination has dried up. As if the proud tower of my genius has collapsed ... Nothing comes ... It is like trying to pick a lock with a wet herring.'[32]

In light of the foregoing discussion, what are we to make of Nunn's *Twelfth Night* as an ironic postmodern production that simultane-ously guarantees the legitimacy of heterosexual relations? The film mobilises notions of the literary text, Shakespeare author-function and history to create a myth of heterosexual romantic love that is stable across the centuries. As Simon Shepherd points out, Shakespeare's life and his texts have become 'national cultural property' and as such academic critics and the film industry construct both the texts and the Shakespeare biography as transcending history rather than being products of the historical process.[33] So, despite disclaimers to the contrary, *Twelfth Night* is not about 'gender-bending' but rather an authorisation of heterosexual romance.

What we find of particular note in this film is the manner in which it rehearses homosexual desire and then disavows it in order to postulate the naturalness and transparency of heterosexual relations. The film's status as a potentially destabilising text in its treatment of sexuality and gender makes it an optimal instance of the rehearsal/disavowal configuration built into its narrative structure. The moments of homoeroticism signify much more than gender-bending titillation. Rather, they represent and enact homosexual desire in order to construct heterosexuality as natural and definitive, drawing attention to the very queerness they are meant to purge. By deconstructing the hetero–homo opposition we can see that not only is the transparency of heterosexuality spurious but it is heterosexuality that is the dependent concept, relying on homosexuality to provide it with its seeming authenticity. Following Harold Beaver's influential essay 'Homosexual Signs' we believe that

> the aim must be to reverse the rhetorical opposition of what is 'transparent' or 'natural' and what is 'derivative' or contrived by demonstrating that the qualities predicated of 'homosexuality' (as a dependent term) are in fact a condition of 'heterosexuality'; that 'heterosexuality', far from possessing a privileged status, must itself be treated as a dependent term.[34]

Given the recent *furor* over Section 28 (actually Section 2A of the 1986 Local Government Act), legislation installed by the Thatcher government that forbids local authorities from intentionally promoting homosexuality and New Labour's 'on message' policy that schools must now positively promote marriage and the family, the mobilisation of England's national author to naturalise hetero-sexuality and erase homosexuality from history seems particularly pernicious. Perhaps it is intellectually naïve to expect the film industry, particularly a film industry in which Hollywood studios are hegemonic, to present us with politically savvy and interesting filmic texts that appeal to the culturally disenfranchised. As Elayne

Tobin has pointedly remarked, to continually assume the posture of being 'gatekeepers of positive representation',[35] cultural critics who expose the bad faith of the film industry are being disingenuous: why, after all, should we expect Hollywood, or the film industry in general, to be sympathetic to our concerns? Tobin offers an important consideration here. However, we believe that cultural critique need not serve merely a negative function. We hope our analysis has demonstrated that Nunn's film contains ideological complexities and ambiguities, demonstrating that every representation contains within itself an oppositional or subversive reading. Though *Twelfth Night* may sound the trumpet of nostalgia for a heterosexual historical past that never was, this representation is always equivocal and will always attempt to cover its tracks. It is in these ghostly footprints that we can find the evidence for a counter-reading that suggests that maybe there is something queer about Shakespeare after all.

Notes

1. For brief consideration of the uses of the Elizabethan London *mise-en-scène* in *Shakespeare in Love*, see Elizabeth Klett's chapter '*Shakespeare in Love* and the end(s) of history' in this volume.
2. Craig Dionne, 'Shakespeare in popular culture: gender and highbrow culture in America', *Genre*, 28 (1995), 385–411, 391.
3. In Deborah Cartmell and Imelda Whelehan (eds), *Adaptations: from text to screen, screen to text* (London: Routledge, 1999), p. 14.
4. 'Postmodernism and consumer culture', *The Anti-Aesthetic: essays on postmodern culture*, ed. Hal Foster (Port Townsend, WA: Pluto Press), 1983, pp. 111–25, 117.
5. Ibid., p. 16
6. Lynn Spigel, 'From the dark ages to the golden age: women's memories and television reruns', *Screen*, 36 (1995), 16–33, 26.
7. Ibid., 28.
8. www.flf.com/twelfth/main.htm
9. Spigel, 25.
10. The latter point is partly rhetorical because the variability in the meaning of Shakespeare can be anecdotally illustrated. The writers of this chapter were driving west on the M5 on Sunday, 23 April 2000 listening to the Easter bank holiday Shakespeare programming on Radio 3 and also discussing Richard Burt's *Unspeakable ShaXXXspeares* (1998). Burt's study is in part

concerned with pornographic representations and uses of Shakespeare in such film productions as *Tromeo and Juliet* (1996), a text which alludes to imagined pornographic interactive CD-ROMs including *As You Lick It, Et Tu Blow Job* and *Much Ado About Humping*. *Tromeo and Juliet* and the middle-brow homage to Shakespeare broadcast on Radio 3 are suggestive of the heterogeneous range of connotations and values signified by the contemporary Shakespeare sign.

11. 'Introduction: Shakespeare the movie', *Shakespeare, the Movie: popularizing the plays on film, TV and video*, eds Lynda Boose and Richard Burt (London: Routledge, 1997), pp. 1–7, 2.
12. Branagh's Hamlet is set in an opulent *fin de siècle* Denmark, while Hoffman's *A Midsummer Night's Dream* is set in late nineteenth-century Italy, complete with the newly invented bicycle as an index to the film's turn-of-the-century setting.
13. *Adaptations*, p. 12
14. Giddings *et al.*, cited in Whelehan, p. 12
15. Spigel, 29.
16. As the final draft of this chapter was finished, Sarah Hall of the *Guardian* reported that Cambridge University was considering demoting the Bard, abolishing the examination paper on Shakespeare to make room for modern literature. Frank Kermode, one of the country's foremost literary critics, quickly responded to this threat against Shakespeare's canonical supremacy, arguing that 'the whole of our literature has to be estimated in relation to him. This [the scrapping of Shakespeare] seems to me a foolishness. It would certainly change the whole balance of the course and would be a net loss to put it mildly.' 3 May 2000, G2, 8.
17. *Guardian*, 3 May, 2000, G2, 1.
18. www.flf.com/twelfth/main.htm
19. www.flf.com/twelfth/main.htm
20. Boose and Burt, p. 16.
21. *The History of Sexuality, Vol. 1: an introduction*, trans. Robert Hurley (London: Allen Lane, 1978), p. 68.
22. Ibid., p. 69.
23. Similarly in *Shakespeare in Love* the truth/sex dyad is enacted through the terms of Queen Elizabeth's wager 'can a play show the very truth and nature of love?' The answer at both the diegetic and extra-diegetic levels is an emphatic 'yes'. Shakespeare as universal literary genius can reproduce the nature of love because he himself has felt it, and this itself is an

anachronistic projection of Romantic expressive ideology. And, more importantly perhaps, Shakespeare can demonstrate the 'very truth and nature of love' because he is one of us, a modern subject in search of the truth of love (for 'love' read 'heterosexual love'), the truth of which will also reveal something about himself. For further discussion of *Shakespeare in Love*'s satirical treatment of Freudian tropes, see Elizabeth Klett's chapter in this volume.

24. Richard Burt, *Unspeakable ShaXXXspeares: queer theory and American kiddie culture* (New York: St Martin's Press, 1998), p. 177.
25. Ibid., p. 177.
26. Judith Butler, *Gender Trouble: feminism and the subversion of identity* (New York: Routledge, 1990), p. 33.
27. Burt, p. 178.
28. Simon Shepherd, 'Shakespeare's private drawer: Shakespeare and homosexuality', *The Shakespeare Myth,* ed. Graham Holderness (Manchester: Manchester University Press, 1988), pp. 96–110, 96.
29. The text used is *The Riverside Shakespeare,* ed. G. Blakemore Evans (Boston: Houghton Mifflin, 1974). Further references are incorporated into the text.
30. Burt, p. 179.
31. Interestingly, there is a corresponding scene in Madden's *Shakespeare in Love* in which Will and Thomas-Viola are observed by a third person, the boatman as voyeur. For a fuller description of this scene, see Klett in this volume. To Klett's description we want to add that, like Feste, the boatman legitimates heterosexuality precisely to the extent that he functions as a voyeur. In fact, the playwright as voyeur is enacted in a comic manner by the young John Webster whose pubescent sexual desire is articulated through an economy of espionage, sadism and bloody spectacle. Here any notion of perversity is displaced onto the comic figure of the young Webster whose later cultural production will enact the dark night of the Jacobean soul as opposed to the 'golden age' of Elizabethan courtly heterosexuality.
32. Klett, above, p. 34.
33. Shepherd, p. 99.
34. Harold Beaver, 'Homosexual signs', *Critical Inquiry*, 8 (1981), 99–119, 115.
35. Elayne Tobin, 'Coffee talk', *Meditations*, 19 (1995), 67–75, 72.

5

Black Rams Tupping White Ewes: Race vs. Gender in the Final Scene of Six *Othellos*

Pascale Aebischer

Othello, Act V scene ii. The ending of this tragedy, with its murder of Desdemona by Othello and Othello's subsequent suicide, is justly famous. However, what really happens in this scene according to the text as it has come down to us in its Folio version has been somewhat obscured by centuries of theatrical choices. Four points in particular have been blurred by stage history. First, Desdemona's murder is clearly meant to happen in full view of the audience, probably on a centre-stage bed,[1] and her body is to remain visible till the bed-curtains are drawn at the end. A witness account of a production in 1610 tells us that much.[2] Secondly, Othello probably smothers Desdemona with his hands, and not with a pillow.[3] Visually, the murder is more brutal than stage history would have us believe, and it is also more physically intimate. Thirdly, Desdemona vigorously defends herself verbally and perhaps also physically. It is obvious that she is very hard to kill, for she revives at least twice before she finally dies both denouncing and forgiving Othello. Her determined re-definition of Othello's 'sacrifice' as a 'murder' leaves no doubt about Othello's guilt and her innocence. Fourthly, the dying Emilia demands to be laid by her mistress's side, and there is no reason why this request would not have been honoured on the Jacobean stage. The final tableau of the play might then have been that of a dying Othello lying down between the two dead women in an attempt to substitute his bond of marriage to their bond of friendship. Or he could have lain down at Desdemona's other side, 'sharing' her with Emilia. Whichever the choice, Othello has to share his status as tragic hero with two female characters.

The scene as mapped in the Folio text and acted on the Jacobean stage was obviously too disturbing for later generations of actors and theatregoers. As a result, the murder scene became the object of numerous revisions in both text and stagings – the most notorious being Talma's temporary introduction of a happy ending, with Desdemona's father rushing in at the last minute to save his daughter.[4] More frequently and consistently, the murder was simply hidden behind the bed-curtains. These revisions all sought the same effects: a toning-down of the eroticism and brutality of the murder, and a carefully stage-managed up-staging of Desdemona and Emilia by Othello. Both these goals must be seen in relationship to the ideologies that shaped eighteenth- and nineteenth-century theatre, for they are as much the result of the decorum demanded by the audiences as a side-effect of the theatre's star-system. The 'racial scandal' of the audience at seeing a black man murdering a white woman could be appeased by hiding that murder,[5] while such a staging also directed the gaze away from the spectacle of the dying/dead woman onto the male star.[6] Not surprisingly, nineteenth-century Desdemonas in general did not put up much resistance to their murderers.

This type of representation was accompanied by the 'discovery' that Othello is not really black at all, but 'white', a 'tawny Moor',[7] and not Thomas Rymer's 'villainous Black-amoor'.[8] What emerged in Victorian stagings, then, was a correlation between race and brutality: the more toned down and effaced the scenes of domestic violence were, the more civilised, 'white', was the Othello represented. Conversely, in keeping with Darwinist theories of criminal atavism as propagated by Caesar Lombroso,[9] the most violent Othellos of the late nineteenth century exhibited features that linked them to the earlier stages of evolution. Thus Tommaso Salvini, the most notoriously ferocious Othello, had a tiger-like walk and an erotic sensuality together with a brutality which one viewer explicitly identified as indicative of 'the taint of savage ancestry'.[10] Salvini's portrayal of the murder, which provoked much protest and admiration, was correspondingly crass in its racist physical imagery:

> he drags her to her feet ... grasps her neck and head with his left hand, knotting his fingers in her loose hair, as if to break her neck. With his Italian Desdemona, Piamonti – 'the personification of pitiful, protesting love gradually resolving into speechless terror' – he pounced upon her, lifted her into the air, dashed with her ... across the stage and through the curtains, which fell behind him. You heard a crash as he flung her on the bed, and growls as of a wild beast over his prey.[11]

Two things here are particularly worthy of attention. First, only an Italian actor, who was himself somewhat lower on the evolutionary scale than his British counterparts, could portray such a convincing image of black male sexuality gone awry. Secondly, this staging very obviously foregrounds Othello and quite literally pushes Desdemona into the background behind the bed-curtains. This is a scene designed for a male star.

It is sobering to see that twentieth-century film productions of the play have found it hard to leave this racist and misogynist heritage behind. Not only the stage and film practitioners but also literary critics have found the play, and in particular its climax, difficult to interpret. Thus modern critics either decry the tragedy as inescapably racist in its production of 'the black man as violent "other"',[12] or they praise it for 'court[ing] a racist impulse ... only to explode such a response'.[13] On screen, these alternative positions quite literally colour the representations in the make-up or skin colour of the actor playing Othello, and the ideological project of the production team rarely fails to be particularly obvious in the final scene of violence. Probably in no other play by Shakespeare is there such a clear relationship between ideology and representation, and no other scene so disturbingly imposes a choice between race and gender. Directorial decisions force audiences to see the killing of Desdemona as either a murder or a sacrifice, to condemn Othello or to excuse his act.[14]

The choice made by Orson Welles in his 1952 film is obvious.[15] Welles's make-up hardly darkens his skin, and his status as both director and star unmistakably shapes his interpretation of the play. Othello cannot but be a light-skinned man whose murder of his wife must seem somewhat heroic and justified. Desdemona, under his direction, becomes little more than a book to write whore on, and her role is a blank which is filled by three different actresses.[16] Her part is much reduced, and the bright light that thematically accompanies her appearances dehumanises her,[17] transforming her into an icon. In the paradigm set up by Laura Mulvey,[18] we can say that she is represented as the object of a male gaze that can at times be fetishising (the scene of the consummation of the marriage) or be characterised by sadistic voyeurism. An example of the latter is the camera's adoption of Othello's viewpoint for his slap of Desdemona in front of the ambassadors. So much do camera and director take Othello's viewpoint that the murder is preceded by a little extratextual proof of Desdemona's capacity for falsehood: she is only *pretending* to be asleep when Othello comes in to kill her. The method he uses for the murder further emphasises the film's dichotomy of male gaze vs. female immobilised object of the gaze: Othello kills Desdemona by pulling a gauze over her face, thus impeding her sight, while his own crazed eyes move closer to her face until he covers her mouth with his, suffocating her with a kiss. The slowness of the killing, its obvious eroticism, and Desdemona's panic-stricken collaboration in the last instants turn what began as a typical horror film scenario (with the camera taking the victim's point of view, showing the intrusion of the killer in the shape of Othello's shadow on the bed curtains) into a sacrifice with a consenting victim.[19] Predictably, Desdemona's last lines are spoken gently, forgivingly, before she almost disappears from the film altogether to make room for Othello's tragic end. It is telling that for Othello's suicide, his face in close-up (no trace of Desdemona can be seen although he is supposedly holding her in his arms) appears light against the dark background. He commits suicide on the line 'threw a pearl away richer than all his tribe, / Set you down this'. By cutting and altering Othello's last few lines, the racist implications of the suicide, in which 'white' Venetian Othello kills his black 'Turkish' self, are avoided. Welles's light-skinned Othello dies a heroic 'honourable murderer' guilty only of 'lov[ing] ... too well' (V.ii.291, 342), with his Desdemona's protest that 'That death's unnatural that kills for loving' quite forgotten (V.ii.42).

Laurence Olivier, under John Dexter's direction in 1964, in a National Theatre production that was converted into a television film,[20] made a different choice for his interpretation of the protagonist, while similarly to Welles making sure that his Othello would not be upstaged by Desdemona in the murder scene. His Othello is a quite appalling projection of racist stereotypes. Encouraged by Leavis's perception of Othello as fundamentally flawed, Olivier looked for defects in the character. He carefully coloured his whole body black and 'othered' most aspects of his characterisation. He used a huge cross around his neck, which he tore off at the point when Othello vows revenge, to create a clear symbolism of surface Christianity and civilisation which barely manages to hide the character's underlying savagery. Olivier's Othello is a direct descendant of Salvini's in their representation of racial otherness. His Othello is characterised by an odd, wide-legged bare-footed gait, extravagant gestures, a vulgar, open-mouthed, lip-smacking laugh, and an inclination to sensuality emblematised in his first appearance, when we see him sniffing a rose. Apparently, Olivier's insistence 'upon a potent sexuality, more highly charged because of Othello's blackness' was 'deliberately meant to be shocking'.[21]

The man who kills Desdemona, then, is a savage who does not need much prompting to yield to his primitive impulses. But he is also acted by a star, and therefore could not possibly be repulsive to the end. The fact that in spite of his racist interpretation and a strong Desdemona in Maggie Smith Olivier eventually managed to win the pity of the audience had as much to do with Olivier's magisterial acting as with subtle cutting and *mise-en-scène*.[22] This begins with the deletion of Emilia's monologue about the marital double standard in Act IV scene iii, which means that Desdemona is sent to her death without an ideological framework of resistance in which to read that death. Incidentally, the suppression of Emilia's monologue also has the side-effect of representing Desdemona's abuse by her husband as happening only within a racially mixed marriage, so that there is no sense of a continuum of domestic abuse stretching from white to mixed households. In the murder scene itself, Desdemona defends herself only verbally. This allows Olivier to tone down the physical violence he displayed in the 'brothel' scene. As a result the murder is very controlled. Furthermore, probably influenced by Welles, the second killing of Desdemona – having smothered her with a pillow first – is represented as a kiss while strangling her, thus underlining the reading of the murder as an act of love. This interpretation is increasingly emphasised throughout the remainder of the play, where Othello's grief at his loss is overwhelming, easily upstaging the killing of Emilia and his stabbing of Iago. He speaks his final monologue with Desdemona held firmly in his arms, his cheek against hers. Famously (and oddly appropriately), Olivier's make-up at this point smudges Smith's cheek, literally blackening her in the process of 'whitening' his crime. Although her body is in the foreground, her face is turned away from the viewer, so that the focus is fully on Othello's weeping face as he pulls a pin out of his bracelet and pierces his throat. How well the re-casting of the murderer into the tragic lover has worked in this film can be seen from the fact that it is one of the rare productions in which the line 'The object poisons sight, / Let it be hid' refers to Iago and not the 'tragic loading of this bed' (V.ii.362–63, 361), which instead becomes the object of the camera's last shot.

Probably the Olivier/Dexter interpretation was eventually felt to be too racially offensive, for when Jonathan Miller directed his BBC/Time-Life production of the tragedy in 1981,[23] Anthony Hopkins's Othello was anything but a white man in blackface. It is difficult to describe which race Hopkins's Othello is actually meant to belong to – to me, he looked very much like a blue-eyed white man with a slight suntan and a bad need for a haircut. I will not dwell on this production because its ideological project can be easily grasped. The accusation of racist stereotyping is very elegantly avoided by making Othello a white man, even if the play's references to his blackness become rather pointless. Othello's violence is not a result of his racial otherness but rather of his violent phallic sexuality as symbolised by the most extravagantly prominent codpiece imaginable. Tellingly, it is this object which hides his final weapon, and his suicide has been described by Lynda Boose as 'a self-emasculation that tropes itself by reflexively figuring the phallus as both aggressor/agent and victim of its own aggressions'.[24] Domestic violence is not the result of racially mixed marriages but rather of male voyeurism and phallic sexuality. Desdemona is, as usual, pushed into the background, to the extent that her death is visible only as a reflection in a mirror. While this representation effectively emphasises the viewer's implication in the male characters' voyeurism, it just as effectively and literally diminishes Desdemona's stature.[25]

Such an evasion of the issue of race in the play could not go on forever in the climate of the 1980s.[26] In 1988, Janet Suzman produced a television version of her Johannesburg Market Theatre production with the black South African actor John Kani in the lead.[27] This film consciously sets itself against its heritage. Quotations from previous productions, such as Olivier's entrance sniffing a rose, are used to create a critical distance from those interpretations. How self-consciously political and critical Suzman's film is can be seen from the fact that she introduced its screening on Channel 4 with a documentary about the production's political South African context. Her statement in the documentary that 'the play addresses the notion of apartheid four hundred years before the epithet was coined – and rejects it' reflects a certain anxiety in the production to prevent misunderstanding and condition the audience into seeing the tragedy as a vindication of miscegenation and Othello as a character driven to murder by Iago's Afrikaans racist discourse. The anti-racist reading is emphasised throughout in

Desdemona's obvious erotic attraction to Othello, which is mirrored by Cassio's affection for his general. Othello himself is characterised by love and attention directed at Desdemona, Cassio and, most touchingly, also at the aged Brabantio. Iago's racism and insinuations, then, disrupt a haven of 'colour-blind' mutual affection. Iago's annihilation of beauty is epitomised in his destruction of the daffodils Cassio had offered Desdemona. The fact that Iago, and not Othello, is the evil character in the play is never in doubt.

The production's ideological project is most clearly evident in Othello's murder itself. His kiss wakes the sleeping Desdemona, who reaches up to him to pull him towards her. Throughout her protestations of innocence she strokes him, and later clings to him as he is straddling her. When finally he puts the pillow over her face to smother her, her hands stroke his arms until her strength abandons her and they sink back down lifelessly. Othello's grief at her death is immediate and devastating – in this portrayal, killing Desdemona is equivalent to killing a part of himself, the murder with Desdemona's consent becoming a sacrifice on the altar of racism.[28] But sexual violence does not disappear from the production altogether. Instead, it is displaced onto two earlier scenes. In the first of these, Othello, having rejected Desdemona's offered handkerchief, violently grabs her, kisses her, and strokes her body passionately, to her utter confusion. The murder in its gentleness hence figures as a conscious rejection of such 'primitive' sexual violence.[29] The promise of sexual violence the play contains so obviously is in this production realised not in the murder of Desdemona but, just before it, in the gang-rape of Bianca by a group of white soldiers.[30] Suzman's film, which aims at representing a black Othello as a noble man and mixed marriages as positive, transfers its sexual violence onto a group of white men with a white victim. 'Whitening' Othello seems to require a 'blackening' of the white characters, especially of Iago who takes great pleasure from Bianca's gang-rape. How completely sexual violence is here displaced from Othello to Iago emerges in Othello's wounding of Iago. This is represented as a castration, blaming the tragedy on *white* male sexuality in an amazing reversal of traditional racist anxieties.[31] Although in this instance such a consistent displacement of sexual violence onto the white male characters, and the representation of Desdemona's murder as a loving sacrifice, work, the sheer effort necessary to make this interpretation convincing reveals that this reading is somewhat forcing the play against its grain. Certainly, the film's emphasis on race pushes gender relations into the background, and female resistance to male violence is restricted to the characters of Emilia and Bianca. Desdemona is a willing victim.

One year after Suzman's film and stage production, another stage production with a black actor in the lead was converted into a television film. I am referring to the RSC production directed by Trevor Nunn, with the opera singer Willard White in the title role, Ian McKellen as Iago, Imogen Stubbs as Desdemona, and Zoë Wanamaker as Emilia.[32] My enumeration of the cast list is deliberate, for both production and film approached the tragedy not as a vehicle for a single star but as a play designed for a company. As a result, the characters of Desdemona and Emilia are revealed to be much stronger than is commonly assumed, and their friendship, which culminates in Emilia's death for the sake of Desdemona, is intense and moving. In this film, as in Suzman's, Emilia is undoubtedly an abused wife, so that she is represented as an effective foil for Desdemona. Although Willard White is a black actor, so that the issue of race is not evaded, the production manages to convey that Othello's violence is not contingent on his race. Instead, it is represented as the result of male peer-pressures and the sexual insecurity of an older man with a young bride. Desdemona is a painful intruder in the homosocial world of the army, in which male bonding takes precedence over heterosexual love. This interpretation, with its emphasis on male peer-pressure and the threat of emasculation, gives added weight to Othello's assertion that Desdemona 'must die, else she'll betray more men' (V.ii.6).

Predictably, Nunn's film, with its emphasis on the disruption of the marital relationship and its strong Desdemona, has a very powerful murder scene. The mood for this is set early on in the willow scene, with a beautiful, gentle intimacy and harmony between Emilia and Desdemona that barely manages to cover up both the women's distress at the breakdown of Desdemona's marriage. Significantly, in the street scene that follows, Othello's brief appearance is not cut (as in the other films and most productions) but rather emphasised. He is straddling Cassio's body when delivering the lines in which he acknowledges Iago's teaching and the concomitant need to kill Desdemona. Peer-pressure makes its last appearance in the context of discordant public violence. As a contrast, the sense of ritual and control at the beginning of the actual murder scene are conveyed strongly through Othello's entrance wearing an exotic white robe and carrying a scimitar.[33] But the order and ritual which Othello is trying to impose on his act, both through his ceremonial costume and his rigid impersonality when answering Desdemona's questions, break down under her resistance. She shatters his control, forcing Othello to commit a disturbingly messy murder. Nunn makes his Desdemona fight Othello with all her might, alternately crying and shouting at him. She even tries to escape, but finds that Othello has locked the door. Finally, he flings her on the bed and lowers himself onto her, his hand covering her mouth. It takes a long time before she goes limp and he rolls off to lie beside her on his back. What we witness is more the climax of a rape-snuff film than a sacrifice. Later, when Emilia is in the room, Desdemona revives with a horrible cry. The camera's close-up on the face of the dying woman makes clear who has won the struggle for the last word. Emilia's death, although once more she is not allowed her place on Desdemona's bed, is given its full weight. Race or male heroism, in Nunn's production, do not overshadow the women's struggle, and gender relations – both heterosexual and homosocial – are shown to be the cause of the 'tragic loading of this bed' (V.ii.361). Furthermore, although it is clear from Iago's cold-blooded stare at the dead bodies that *he* is the villain of the piece, no one who has witnessed this particular murder will be able to excuse it glibly. Under Trevor Nunn's elegant direction the murder is neither the result of race (Dexter/Olivier) or racism (Suzman/Kani), nor is it motivated by sadistic and voyeuristic male phallic sexuality gone awry (Welles, Miller/Hopkins). By allowing the company to explore the gender relations as scripted in Shakespeare's play, Nunn has shown that an emphasis on gender relations might be the solution to the problems of racism posed by the tragedy.

It is the more surprising and disappointing that only six years after Nunn's sensitive and intelligent production, the pendulum seems to have swung back in Oliver Parker's feature film adaptation of *Othello*.[34] Parker's casting of African American actor Laurence Fishburne in the lead – the first black actor to play Othello on the big screen – superficially suggests an awareness of the tragedy's racial dimension. On closer view, however, the film appears to be ultimately more racist than its predecessors. While earlier white actors in blackface were obvious impersonators of racial otherness, so that race was clearly a performance, Parker more insidiously appropriates Fishburne's body to naturalise the film's racist interpretation. As if Fishburne's body were not black enough, Parker uses jewellery and tattoos to mark it as 'other', 'exotic', and 'erotic'.

Parker's desire to emphasise the 'passion and romance' of the relationship between Othello and Desdemona results in a representation of both their bodies as fetishised objects of an eroticising gaze.[35]
An early flashback to their courtship shows Desdemona less
enthralled by Othello's narrative than by the tattoos on his hand
and head. A later shot of Othello seen through Desdemona's eyes
focuses on his crotch as he is unfastening his belt, reducing his
attraction to exotic sexuality in a way that, in its re-enforcement of
racist stereotypes, stands in stark contrast to Suzman's portrayal of
the couple's eroticism. Both lovers in Parker's film are, in fact,
'othered' in a way that poses serious questions about the policies
governing the film's casting. While the Franco-Swiss Irene Jacob's
talent as an actor is not in doubt, her accent at crucial moments
becomes an insurmountable obstacle. This and the drastic cuts of
her lines (she hardly gets a chance to plead for Cassio) undermine
the very eloquence that, in both the Quarto and Folio playtexts, is a
major reason for Othello's suspicions and jealousy.[36] The
consequent focus on her body, which is underlined by shots of her
adultery with Cassio as fantasised by Othello, debases both her and
Othello, whose obsession with sex is thus exposed while the
audience has been given all the visual proof it needs to condemn
Desdemona.

With Desdemona thus 'bewhored', identified as 'other' and
silenced by her accent, and Othello similarly fetishised and reduced
to his sexuality, the audience is perversely invited to share Iago's
point of view. As played by Kenneth Branagh, Iago is not only the
bearer of the gaze and the controller of what the film spectator is
allowed to see,[37] but as one of the film's few competent speakers of
RP and Shakespearean verse, his words carry the greatest authority.[38]
Whereas Ian McKellen's strong Iago in Nunn's production had
resulted in an exposure of domestic violence and the strength of peer
pressure, Branagh's Iago spends most of the film in an ugly
competition with Othello and Desdemona, a struggle from which
he emerges as a winner in the final scene. There, Othello is racialised
more than ever through his costume and the cleansing ritual he
performs before the murder. While Desdemona's pleas are disabled
by her increasingly thick accent, her vehement physical struggle
against Fishburne's muscular and savagely violent Othello is doomed
to be ineffectual from the start. He smothers her with a pillow,
erasing both her face and her speech. Significantly, Othello makes
only one attempt at killing her, Desdemona's last lines are cut, and

the camera focuses on Othello's face as Desdemona's fighting hand becomes loving, stroking his face in silent acceptance of her death at his hands. As in Welles's film, where Desdemona was only pretending to be asleep, Parker first taints Jacob's Desdemona through her nude scenes with Cassio before erasing her almost entirely from the film. Unlike Welles's Othello who benefited from this erasure, however, Fishburne is not left at the centre of attention for long. In Parker's heavily cut script, both Othello and Emilia are quickly upstaged by Iago, who once more appropriates language and the camera that follows him in his escape from the room in which, to Parker's credit, the dying Emilia is sharing Desdemona's deathbed. When Iago is brought back to the bedchamber, the main focus is on him. Othello's gaze is locked in Iago's even while he is talking to Cassio. The camera neglects the women's bodies on the bed until Othello commits suicide and painfully pulls himself up to the obscured Desdemona for his final kiss. A reaction shot shows a flash of genuine emotion across the face of Iago who, at the end of the scene, crawls halfway up to Othello's body on the bed, resting his head on Othello's knee while triumphantly staring at the camera. When Cassio opens the window to let the sunlight in, the film's final shot of the bed emblematises its interpretation of the tragedy: in the foreground Iago is lying on the legs of the centrally positioned Othello, whose body is partly covering Desdemona on his left. Barely within the frame on the left lies Emilia. Despite Fishburne's powerful performance, in the *Othello* of the 1990s, Iago is the hero and wielder of the racist and misogynist gaze that has reduced Othello and Desdemona to their physicality and disabling 'otherness'. Played by a real black man and a real white woman and thus using the racial and gendered casting that had produced Nunn's sensitive reading, Parker's film disturbingly attempts to naturalise racial and sexual inferiority by showing it to be embodied, not performed as on the early modern stage.

Notes

1. For the centrality of Desdemona's bed, see E.K. Chambers, *The Elizabethan Stage*, Vol. 3 (Oxford: Clarendon Press, 1923), pp. 112–14 and Peter Thomson, *Shakespeare's Theatre* (London: Routledge, 1992), p. 52.
2. Henry Jackson's account of the production he saw in Oxford in 1610 mentions that 'although she [Desdemona] pleaded her

case very effectively throughout, yet moved [us] more after she was dead, when, lying on her bed, she entreated the pity of the spectators by her very countenance' (quoted by Dympna Callaghan, *Woman and Gender in Renaissance Tragedy: a study of 'King Lear', 'Othello', 'The Duchess of Malfi' and 'The White Devil'* (New York: Harvester Wheatsheaf, 1989), p. 90).

3. This can be inferred from Othello's assertion to Gratiano that 'these hands have newly stopped [Desdemona's breath]' (V.ii.200). All quotations from *Othello* are from the Folio text and refer to the line numbering and spellings of E.A.J. Honigmann's Arden 3 edition (Walton-on-Thames: Nelson & Sons Ltd, 1997).

4. Marvin Rosenberg, *The Masks of Othello: the search for the identity of Othello, Iago, and Desdemona by three centuries of actors and critics* (Berkeley: University of California Press, 1961), p. 32.

5. Michael Neill, 'Unproper beds: race, adultery, and the hideous in *Othello*', *Shakespeare Quarterly*, 40 (1989), 386.

6. James R. Siemon, '"Nay, that's not next": *Othello*, V.ii in Performance, 1760–1900', *Shakespeare Quarterly*, 37 (1986), p. 47.

7. Carol Jones Carlisle, *Shakespeare from the Greenroom: actors' criticisms of four major tragedies* (Chapel Hill: University of North Carolina Press, 1969), p. 192.

8. Thomas Rymer, 'From *A Short View of Tragedy* (1603)', in *Shakespeare: 'Othello': a casebook*, ed. John Wain (London: Macmillan, 1994), p. 42.

9. Caesar Lombroso and William Ferrero, *The Female Offender* (London: T. Fisher Unwin, 1895).

10. Quoted in Rosenberg, *The Masks of Othello*, p. 112.

11. Ibid., p. 113.

12. Jyotsna Singh, 'Othello's identity, postcolonial theory, and contemporary African rewritings of *Othello*', in *Women, 'Race', and Writing in the Early Modern Period*, eds Margo Hendricks and Patricia Parker (London: Routledge, 1994), p. 291.

13. Martin Orkin, 'Othello and the "plain face" of racism', *Shakespeare Quarterly*, 38 (1987), 176.

14. The third option, which would be to follow Desdemona's ambiguous example and forgive Othello, is made problematic by the patronising superiority it implies on the part of the forgiver.

15. *Othello*. Dir. Orson Welles. Perf. Orson Welles, Suzanne Cloutier, Michaèl MacLiammòir, Fay Compton. [Mercury, 1952] Re-edited re-release: Castle Hill Productions, 1992.
16. Virginia Mason Vaughan, *'Othello': a contextual history* (Cambridge: Cambridge University Press, 1994), p. 205.
17. Ibid., p. 207.
18. 'Visual pleasure and narrative cinema', in *Visual and Other Pleasures* (Bloomington: Indiana University Press, 1989), pp. 14–38.
19. In horror films, '[t]he action is inevitably seen from the victim's point of view; we stare at the door (wall, car roof) and watch the surface open to first the tip and then the shaft of the weapon.' Carol J. Clover, *Men, Women and Chain Saws: gender in the modern horror film* (Princeton: Princeton University Press, 1992), p. 31.
20. *Othello*. Dir. John Dexter. Perf. Laurence Olivier, Maggie Smith, Frank Finlay, Joyce Redman. National Theatre/British Home Entertainment, 1964.
21. Carlisle, *Shakespeare from the Greenroom*, p. 197.
22. Ibid., p. 198.
23. *Othello*. Dir. Jonathan Miller. Perf. Anthony Hopkins, Penelope Wilton, Bob Hoskins, Rosemary Leach. BBC/Time-Life, 1981.
24. 'Grossly gaping viewers and Jonathan Miller's *Othello*', in *Shakespeare, the Movie: popularizing the plays on film, TV and Video*, eds Lynda E. Boose and Richard Burt (London: Routledge, 1997), p. 194.
25. For an excellent discussion of this film's play on Othello's and the viewer's voyeurism, see Boose, 'Grossly gaping viewers', pp. 192ff.
26. I am not including a discussion of Liz White's 1980 film of *Othello*, which was never commercially released and which I have therefore not been able to see. The film, which was made by an all-black production crew and cast, is certainly worthy of detailed analysis, as Peter S. Donaldson has shown in *Shakespearean Films / Shakespearean Directors* (Boston: Unwin Hyman, 1990).
27. *Othello*. Dir. Janet Suzman. Perf. John Kani, Joanna Weinberg, Richard Haddon Haines, Dorothy Gould. Market Theatre/Othello Productions, Focus Films, and Portobello Productions, 1988.

28. See Deborah Cartmell, 'Shakespeare, film and race: screening *Othello* and *The Tempest*', in *Interpreting Shakespeare on Screen* (London: Macmillan, 2000), p. 74 for a reading of Suzman's interpretation as inadvertently racist.

29. This contrast between earlier (sexual) violence and gentleness in the murder scene is another instance of Suzman's intertextual engagement with the Dexter/Olivier production and TV film.

30. Suzman recalls that '[a]t *that point in the play, a feeling of gross sexual anarchy seemed a priority as an image*' (personal communication, 1 October 1998, her emphasis).

31. Barbara Hodgdon, 'Race-ing *Othello*, re-engendering white-out', in *The Shakespeare Trade: performances and appropriations* (Philadelphia: University of Pennsylvania Press), p. 49 reads the castration as 'not only reversing power relations between black and white bodies but literally enacting an even deeper political and social fear of white disempowerment'.

32. *Othello*. Dir. Trevor Nunn. Perf. Willard White, Imogen Stubbs, Ian McKellen, Zoë Wanamaker. The Other Place/Primetime, 1989.

33. In a film that throughout avoids the charge of racism by foregrounding marital violence in both mixed and white couples and by portraying a black Othello who is thoroughly 'white' in everything but his skin, this choice of costume unfortunately opens up a possibility for a racist reading of the murder through the implication that it is Othello's African self who chooses to kill his wife. This change of costume, albeit impressive in its evocation of ritual, is moreover paradoxical in view of Othello's own perception that he is about to perform a sacrifice for the sake of 'white' male solidarity – rather than an emancipation from white male culture, Othello sees his act as what will seal his alliance to that culture.

34. *Othello*. Dir. Oliver Parker. Perf. Laurence Fishburne, Irene Jacob, Kenneth Branagh, Anna Patrick. Castle Rock Entertainment, 1995. For discussions of this film that set it in the context of the O.J. Simpson trial, see Hodgdon, 'Race-ing *Othello*' and Cartmell, 'Shakespeare, film and race'.

35. Parker as quoted by Hodgdon, 'Race-ing *Othello*', p. 67.

36. The casting of the young Fishburne removes another textual reason for Othello's jealousy. As a result, all of the lines referring

to the age difference between Othello and Desdemona are cut from the film's script.

37. At one point, Iago blocks the camera lens with his hand, an action that is read by Hodgdon as 'less a means of keeping viewers from looking at him than a way of controlling what they see, his gesture knowingly marks him as the film's "true" author, in control of both Shakespeare's text and the camera' ('Race-ing *Othello*', p. 70).

38. Most Venetians are 'othered' and disabled by their accents, leaving linguistic power in the hands of the two RSC veterans Branagh and Michael Maloney (Roderigo).

6

Cool Intentions: The Literary Classic, the Teenpic and the 'Chick Flick'

Sarah Neely

Retrovision is a 'vision into or of the past' and implies an act of possessing the ability to read the past, in the way that one would possess a prophetic vision. Like 'retrospect', it involves casting a backward glance from the vantage point of the present, from the privileged perspective that allows one 'to look back ... [and establish] a review of past events'.[1] The idea of the retrospect can hardly avoid a reinterpretation, or a 'revisioning' of what is being looked back on.

Cruel Intentions, Robert Kumble's 1999 film version of Choderlos de Laclos' eighteenth-century epistolary novel *Les Liaisons dangereuses*,[2] in common with other recent films such as *Clueless* and Baz Luhrmann's *William Shakespeare's Romeo + Juliet* (1996), represents the recent popularity of the teenpics's confident reappropriation of historical and canonical texts, and is evidence of a culture's obsession with looking back. All of these films emerge from a history of films targeted to a youth market, which, Thomas Doherty has suggested, marked its beginnings in 1955.[3] Emerging as another form of the exploitation film, Doherty denotes the teenpic genre as involving a heavy-handed approach to marketing which has influenced and is carried on in today's production environment.[4] He defines the teenpic genre as a 'product of the decline of the classical Hollywood cinema and the rise of the privileged American teenager'.[5] In short, youth had the money to become the dominant cinema-goers of the 1950s market.

In the eyes of industry, they were most notable for their power as consumers and the development of an appeal to this newly found 'subculture'[6] would ultimately involve the creation of films which reflected the characteristics of the group itself. Within any culture the acknowledgement of a group's existence within the sphere of popular culture offers solidarity and validates their own identity.

Thus, because they were now the customers and held market power, the youth 'subculture' would be given the images they wanted to see. However, as Doherty points out, the 'subculture' was only representative of the privileged youth, which the market most often deemed to be primarily male. Doherty describes the exploitation strategies of the mid-1960s as having developed into what was described as 'The Peter Pan Syndrome', which held its main target as the nineteen-year-old male. It depended on the fact that a girl would watch anything a boy would watch, but that a boy would not watch something a girl would.[7] This strategy would suggest that the teenage girl was then excluded from any considerations of the filmic content or marketing. As Doherty later explains a 'she' was never considered within the framework of the 'juvenile delinquent', yet as the market looked for cleaner, more morally appropriate images of youth, the female depiction proved to be more palatable. The female then came to the forefront of representation as the embodiment of the morally upright young person. Arguably the teenpics produced in the 1990s are confronting these representations in an attempt to break away from the previous portrayals of femininity.

Teenpics arising from the last decade share a thematic mix which addresses issues of sex and class, and deal with traditional themes of the relationship of youth to authority (either the family or educational institution). Various media are related intertextually and films are made from television series and vice versa: for example, *Clueless* the film becomes a TV series. Additionally the various media trade popular stars. Buffy the vampire slayer becomes the evil, scheming, step-sister Kathryn Merteuil in *Cruel Intentions* (1999). The actress, Sarah Michelle Geller, even makes a brief, hardly recognisable cameo appearance in the film *10 Things I Hate About You* (1999). Popular music is incorporated into films or is composed especially for a new film. Clips from the films are then arranged and displayed as music videos which appear on MTV. MTV also funds and advertises its own brand of films designed to reach its own viewers and so the boundaries blur. Still representing the largest segment of viewers, teens continue to be targeted as a viable market, but as the babyboomers grow older, it is necessary to avoid exclusion and instead incorporate features into the teenpic that will target the adult consciousness.[8] This necessity is not only represented in the narrative, but also in the soundtracks of teenpics of the 1990s which include songs that the parents of teens will have heard of, but not the teens who are the film's main target.[9] Ultimately the soundtracks become a combination of songs popular with teens from different generations, including the most recent. The teenpics of today leave room for adults to remember their own youth as well as for teens to explore theirs. Indeed youth is no longer framed in relation to adulthood but is, as Johanna Wyn and Rob White detail, a 'symbol of consumption' in a society in which youth is merely the 'outcome of the process of becoming more and more in control over one's body'.[10] Youth, defined as a result of performativity, is made easily at home in the issues surrounding identity present in the contemporary teenpic genre.

Unlike the 'invisible girl' syndrome of the past, described by Michael Brake, Angela McRobbie and Jenny Garber,[11] which represented girls only as distanced possessions of boys, lacking their own sexual independence and identity, the teenpics of today address these very issues. Although teenpics of the 1980s certainly included representations of teenage girls, films such as *Pretty in Pink* (1986), *The Breakfast Club* (1985), *Say Anything* (1989), *Sixteen Candles* (1984), and *Ferris Bueller's Day Off* (1986) did so within the context of the male-dominated teen subculture. Films today rarely alter this format; however, they attempt to address the issues head-on, unashamedly making reference to a teenage girl subculture. As with their 1980s predecessors these films focus on the construction of a socially acceptable, feminine self. The 'makeover' teenpic functions at various levels, but most importantly, in the most recent films, it brings up questions involving the construction of identity and the conflicts at play between past representations of femininity and the demands placed upon women today.

Teenpics from the 1950s have focused on issues of maturity and the transition to adulthood. It is not surprising, then, that today, because of changing political circumstances regarding the role of women, a major focus has come to include the complex transition from girlhood to womanhood, considering that ideas of womanhood are multiple and changing. The 'makeover' teenpic affords the opportunity for these identities to be visually played out, but in accordance with the cultural conventions of our own times, results in the assimilation of an 'awkward' teen into society through the appropriation of acceptable feminine appearance and behaviour. Problematically, the new teenpics seek to represent a female youth culture through the assertion of taste and feminine identity and often such constructions exist only at the surface. In *10 Things I Hate About You* the main protagonist is defined through the clothes she wears, the difficult books she reads and, most importantly, the music she listens to. She herself hopes to form her own band and identifies with the music of other women, music that her peers refer to as 'angry girl music of the indie-rock persuasion' or 'chicks who can't play their instruments'. Music becomes an important defining feature of the personality and even defines one's sexuality: Bianca asserts that she is not a 'K.D. lang fan', and we are immediately meant to deduce by this reference that she is not a lesbian. This is the kind of shorthand representation defining identity in the teenpics of today.

Yet Generation X is noted for its rootless, indefinable qualities and so it must assume a patchwork-like composition of existing cultural texts and ones borrowed from other times. It is the multiplicity and barrage of surface images which come to define identity. Johanna Wyn and Rob White look to Henry Giroux's analysis of youth culture to explore the many layered forms of 'cultural performance, identity and political agency' existent in young adult experience which Giroux had claimed was characteristic of a postmodern youth culture being 'condemned to wander within and between multiple borders and spaces marked by excess, otherness and difference'.[12] This hybridisation becomes recognisable through methods of consumption of the teen films themselves, as well as the representative consumption within them.

The opening sequence of *10 Things I Hate About You* illustrates this. A veteran student is showing the new guy around the school, offering a breakdown of the many groups to watch out for, including the beautiful people, the coffee drinkers, the white rastas, the cowboys, and the future MBAs. What he points out for many of the groups is the superficiality of their named identity: the coffee drinkers are shown with a cup of coffee, the white rastas are only so because they 'smoke a lot of weed', the cowboys' closest connection to cattle is through McDonald's. Ironically, the MBAs had ostracised him from their group because they suspected his Izod (a brand of sports clothing) to be from an outlet mall (a discount designer warehouse), an inauthentic source in their eyes. Identity is entirely formed through appearances and brand names and has little to do with individuality or what is below the surface. In this respect, the teenpic's characteristic movement from adolescence to adulthood is charted out by the ways in which the character adequately negotiates the meanings of various cultural symbols.

One other notable change in recent teen films, remarked upon by Thomas Doherty, is the familial authoritative role. The violence and suicide evident in earlier teen films represented a youth culture's necessity for family intervention and was often structured around a rebellion against that very authority. Today's teenpics, by contrast, involving Generation X characters, differ considerably in that they demonstrate an almost entire lack of authority or intervention from the family.[13] In the films that I shall go on to discuss – *10 Things I Hate About You, She's All That* (1999), *Clueless* (1995) and *Cruel Intentions* – the mother is conspicuously absent. This primarily allows for the female teen protagonist to assemble her identity by herself and may serve as a metaphor for postfeminism; but it additionally generates connotations of the latchkey kid, the parentless child, who must grow up quickly and assume adult roles. As the male protagonist of *Cruel Intentions*, Sebastian is told by his psychiatrist: 'Adolescence is a difficult time and without great parenting things can go awry, but you have to rise above their mistakes.' In all of this, there is a sense that the children are forging new ground entirely on their own, but only *Cruel Intentions* is devoid of any parental intervention. The other films all contain an at least moderately involved father, but the father only increases the speed with which the daughter must attempt to 'grow up' and take on the responsibilities of the household. In these films it is rarely that we see a father attending to domestic chores; instead a gap exists where the daughter must somehow replace the role of the absent mother. This sometimes darkly resonates as a metaphor for the working mother's inadequate presence in the home, and thus appears as a sexist subtext.

Jon Lewis locates teeny-bopper culture in the bedroom of the teenage girl and defines it as comprising a mode of secrecy dedicated to an obsession with stars.[14] Differing from male-dominated youth subcultures, female teenage subculture grew out of private surroundings. Actors pinned up on teenage girls' walls became feminised cultural icons and as 'The Peter Pan Syndrome' suggested, resulted in the male teenage cinemagoer's disdain. Still evident in male teen icons today, the effect seems to have been diluted with the parallel development of their female equivalent. Today's teen icons, both male and female, are all likely pin-ups, not only on teenagers' walls, but within the culture of MTV, the 'official' website, teen magazines and other fanzines, which continue the pleasures of the film far beyond its initial screening. Like the soundtrack, characteristic of these films, they become markers of the teens' own tastes and identity.

Cruel Intentions, 10 Things I Hate About You, She's All That and *Clueless* are all developed from within the teenpic genre and they share numerous characteristics that are unique to this group. In addition to the already mentioned absence of the mother, the distant or workaholic father, alteration of a character's feminine appearance, and the popular soundtrack, there are many other identifying features. Like other films of their kind, they all begin with that exemplary teenage object, the car. Usually set to the contemporary music of the soundtrack, the protagonists enter the frame in their car (usually a convertible) and often their coolness is contrasted with other key characters' not-so-fashionable cars. Accordingly, the female characters also are defined through what they wear and are often shown shopping, all of which accords with the representations of consumption previously suggested. Issues of race, multiculturalism and sexuality are presented tokenistically, manifesting themselves in the same superficial manner as are other forms of identity – such as the ever-present references to PMS, which often act to diffuse the most interesting and complex instances of female identity. Most importantly, all of the above films are adaptations, or are suggestive of 'classic' texts. In corresponding order, they are updates of Choderlos de Laclos' *Les Liaisons dangereuses,* William Shakespeare's *The Taming of the Shrew,* George Bernard Shaw's *Pygmalion* and Jane Austen's *Emma,* and are all reframed in the setting of the teen angst-ridden time of high school. The presence of the original text is faintly identifiable outside of the essential narrative strands. Instead the literary origins surface in character and place names, random lines of dialogue, and the frequent appearance of high-brow, literary classics which develops a commentary of the relations between high and low culture being played out through the filmic text itself.

Even though *Cruel Intentions* is based on an eighteenth-century text, the psychiatrist reminds us in the film's first few opening lines that 'what's in the past is over'. *Les Liaisons dangereuses* is about the end of an era, the end of the comfort of the aristocracy leading up to the French Revolution. The pre-revolutionary decadence lends itself well to the teenpic and surfaces in such details as costuming and set, where the extravagant velvet interiors and corseted characters seem only natural to the genre's preoccupation with the surface. *Cruel Intentions* likewise arises from the schism occurring within feminism and, additionally, the lack of guidance felt by Generation X-ers. In this manner, *Cruel Intentions* appears to be looking back through teen dramas to see where the 'new woman' can be placed.

In other genres such as the horror film, Doherty and critics such as Tania Modleski have noted the punitive approach to female sexuality with the female protagonist often sentenced to death.[15] Only the 'good girl' lives; the sexually active or sexually demonstrative are always killed. Not so obviously, some teen films produce similar effects where 'good' girls are never portrayed as sexual. Although rebellion to the societal construction of female identity is not unfamiliar to the eighteenth-century text, in the film version it is pitted against representations of femininity in the 1960s and 70s through its reference to *The Brady Bunch*. In a pivotal speech, in which Kathryn reveals herself to Sebastian, she claims she is punished because she 'exudes confidence and enjoys sex' and that she has to 'act like Mary Sunshine 24/7 so I can be considered a lady'. She laments the fact that she is 'the Marsha-fucking-Brady of the Upper East Side and sometimes I want to kill myself'. She recognises the fact that female sexuality is attacked vehemently by society and so she plays against it while hiding beneath the mask of its own creation. This is similar to the function of the 'makeover' within the other teenpics that serves to reinvent their characters into society's acceptable degree of femininity.

Fortunately, these images are always rendered superficial and untenable and so hold with them the possibility of future reinventions of self, a practice familiar to teen icons themselves. Madonna, who has most famously reinvented herself on numerous occasions, has been described by E. Ann Kaplan as representative of a 'postmodern feminist stance'.[16] Suggestive of the fluidity of self and other, such reinventions work subversively against societal structures of gendering. In other words, it manages to subvert the punishment inflicted upon those who fail to perform their own gender appropriately. Esther Sonnet's explanation for the surge of modernised adaptations, or 'postmodern historical literary adaptation', in her essay on *Clueless* is that it's a 'symptom of a popular cultural antifeminist articulation of nostalgia for an unchallenged patriarchal order'.[17] Although our culture's desire for the historical remake may be indicative of this, the outcome of these remakes suggests otherwise. Placed within the rubric of the teen genre's male-centred beginnings, the two forms (literary classic and teen film) do not work in opposition, but collaboratively. And, regardless of attempts to centralise the female teen, as Sonnet suggests, these attempts always serve retroactive purposes.

In Wyn and White's 1997 book, the punishment for the 'failure' to perform one's gender to the expectations of society is shown through the experience of a student who is punished for taking power at a time when the school, in its gendered definitions of power, would expect her to be submissive.[18] It is an accurate depiction of the way in which society chastises those, particularly the young, who fail to adhere to the performative definitions of gender. This conflict and necessity for the female teen to become expert at reading and performing the gendered expectations of society is a crucial and central theme in all of the films. The nostalgia within the films may be seen as a pastiche of past representations of femininity which is undermined by the ultimate failure of the 'makeover' to conceal the real person. It is suggestive of the reality that a patriarchal order is still resistant to change, and that greater efforts are needed other than just the odd subversive makeover.

The romance novel offers a useful connection to these particular versions of the teenpic because of their similar functions and contexts. Brenda Daly has suggested that the romance novel offers the teen a 'psychic space' upon which to project their own issues.[19] Film also proffers this 'psychic space' but this act of reading is not entirely tied to the reading of teens in the twentieth century. For centuries, texts have been seen as dangerous because of this way in which they can be read subjectively.

One such example is a Frenchwoman by the name of Marie Cappelle-Lafarge who in 1840 was on trial for poisoning her husband. Because of the novels she chose to read she quickly became an example of how dangerous the government believed certain books to be when read by a woman of a certain disposition.[20] As Jann Matlock points out in her study of Madame Lafarge, the book was believed to have envenomed its readers in an equally deadly manner. Many other books have been implicated or rendered suspect in this way, including *Cruel Intentions*'s source *Les Liaisons dangereuses,* a novel that could also be read in a variety of scandalous ways. As Madame Lafarge's experience proves, reading and writing, especially about issues regarded as private, has always been a dangerous matter. Similarly, arguments surrounding adaptation have identified the ability of a film to give a responsible reading to its audience, which usually implies one that is faithful to the original text. Any instance of rewriting what is deemed to be preserved and protected by this idea of the sacred original may be vehemently opposed and rejected. This curious phenomenon may be likened to other examples of transgressive reading throughout Madame Lafarge's time. In her study, Jann Matlock also refers to women who wrote between the lines of their own books in order to find an outlet of expression for their lives through fictional texts, and refers to Madame Lafarge as a woman who 'writes in the spaces they would use to confine her'.[21] In this way, the text acts as a catalyst necessary for forging a new identity.

The idea of writing one's own text through rewriting another may perhaps be applicable to adaptation and more specifically modernised adaptations. In other words, women wrote their identity in the margins by annotating other texts in the same way that adaptations are themselves annotations. Versions which refuse to simply recreate literature as ultimate truth and instead create them from the accepted viewpoint of their time, incorporating the cultural experience of a particular historical moment, have the potential to present a more subversive representation through the irony created by the gap between remake and original. And, like the much-scorned female reader-turned-writer of the nineteenth century, a contemporary filmmaker who writes his or her own story between the lines of literary classics may often be seen as threatening or dangerous. It may be a difference which, as Jann Matlock suggests by pointing to Roland Barthes's concept of the readerly and writerly text, is dependent on the text itself or, equally possible, solely dependent on the will of the reader.[22]

Even if the reproduction of a cultural text is nostalgically preserved for the representation of an 'unchallenged patriarchal order', a reading, of any textual form, cannot be as easily controlled or moderated. In Henry Jenkins's study of fan culture entitled *Textual Poachers* a similar act to that of women writing between the lines of novels in the nineteenth century in order to assert their own identity is described as existing within various media. In his essay appropriately entitled 'Scribbling in the Margins: Fan Readers/Fan Writers' he describes how television fan writers 'reclaim female experiences from the margins of male-centred texts, offering readers the kinds of heroic women still rarely available elsewhere in popular culture'.[23] Of course, films may also be read in this way, and I would argue that teen films in particular, because of their cultural existence that permeates well beyond the screen into other factions of teen life, generate multiple readings as well as new texts.

A discussion of these issues begs the question: why, if a contemporary film is created to address contemporary issues, is a classic literary text being relied upon to form the basis of the narrative? Not only is this trend evident in the four films mentioned but also in films such as Baz Luhrmann's *Romeo + Juliet* and, most recently, Michael Almereyda's teen update of *Hamlet* (2000), as well as Tim Blake Nelson's teen version of *Othello*, minimally entitled *O* (2000).[24] Such updates may wish to enliven our understanding, or rather that of its teenage audience, of a canonically revered text – the kind of work taught in classrooms everywhere. The teacher in *10 Things I Hate About You* prefaces his own teaching of Shakespeare with the disclaimer: 'I know Shakespeare is a dead white guy, but he knows his shit, so we can overlook that.' Although this would imply that it is the author we are resisting, but not the text, in the filmic updates it is the text *and* the author which are culturally transplanted in the present day. This is similar to Herman Melville's expressed wish for Shakespeare to have lived to walk down Broadway so that it would be possible to see what he would have said without the censorship of the Elizabethan age.[25] In other words, the act of culturally transplanting Shakespeare involves the desire to reanimate him in contemporary times, in ways which Abel Gance anticipated by having 'exclaimed enthusiastically' that 'Shakespeare, Rembrandt, Beethoven will make films – all legends ... await their exposed resurrection'.[26]

Apart from the general cultural implications, each novel generates different forms of irony by culturally transplanting the text to the teenpic genre. *Les Liaisons dangereuses*, because of its epistolary form, surfaces in the film through the appearances of diaries and letters. The letters in Laclos's novel serve as psychological masks for individual characters and are revealed to the reader through a comparison of the letters offering the multiple points of view existing within the liaison. The tension between what is told and what is not, and the construction of each character's public persona through their manipulation of writing is not entirely recreated in *Cruel Intentions*, which seems to include the appearances of journals and letters only to acknowledge its textual origins. However, the letters' role in constructing identity is echoed more profoundly in the film through the alliance with the teen genre's constructions of femininity. Other contemporised films and their textual sources

evoke similar relations of identity. *William Shakespeare's Romeo +
Juliet* is deeply embedded in Shakespeare's play on the construction
of self in relation to family and other forms of naming. The themes
within the novel *Emma* concerning the tenuous nature of
appearances lend themselves well to this particular genre, as do the
similar preoccupations with outward appearances in *The Taming of
the Shrew* and *Pygmalion.*

Within the teenpics themselves, the texts become another method
of appropriating cultural taste and negotiating identity. All of the
films discussed here involve the representation of the texts they are
based on, yet the majority of the films barely acknowledge the texts
from which they have originated. Their names are altered entirely
and the original source is only very briefly referred to in the rapid
succession of opening credits. However, all of them contain
numerous references to other literary texts. Among them are the
writings of Sylvia Plath, Nietszche, Shakespeare, Hemingway.
Highbrow texts are referred to with as much frequency as popular
texts such as MTV, *The Real World*, television commercials, K-Mart,
and the *Brady Bunch.* Symbolic of the importance of contemporary
cultural literacy, in addition to more classical references in today's
teen society, the play of these texts not only represents additional
identity formations but represents the cultural play at work within
the films themselves.

The teenpics themselves become a marker of taste for their
viewers. At many of the fan websites it is a common occurrence to
come across a fan review of the film that begins: 'I liked this film,
but I'm only 15 [or 14, or 16].' Equally common are the hurried
additional remarks: 'but my brother saw it too and he liked it even
though it's a "chick flick"'. Comments such as these which are
encountered on the many fan websites imply that even the con-
stituents of the very market at which the films are primarily targeted
are conscious of what was called in the 1960s 'The Peter Pan
Syndrome'. Although much has happened politically since the
1960s, boys (or just about anyone) would not want to watch, or
admit to want to watch, something a young girl would. The industry
itself seems to have become aware of this, as the films become more
inclusive in their culturally varied soundtracks, marketing
techniques, and more importantly the referencing of the accepted
canonical text. Ultimately, the most truthful reason for adapting a
classical literary text within the teenpic genre is to offer a renewed

attempt to negotiate the complex relations of gendered viewing practices which still persist from the 1960s.

Notes

1. *Oxford English Dictionary*, CD-ROM (Oxford: Oxford University Press, 1992).
2. Choderlos de Laclos, *Les Liaisons dangereuses*, trans. P.W.K. Stone (Harmondsworth: Penguin, 1961).
3. Thomas Doherty, *Teenagers and Teenpics: the juvenilization of American movies in the 1950s* (Boston: Unwin Hyman, 1988), p. 3.
4. Ibid., p. 5.
5. Ibid., p. 14.
6. Although Doherty considers the appropriate use of this word, he clarifies that it is limited to only those who are privileged enough to afford it. See pp. 48–50 for his analysis.
7. Ibid., p. 157.
8. Doherty recognised this characteristic in teenpics of the 1980s such as *Fast Times at Ridgemont High* (1982) and *Risky Business* (1983) which he felt were marketed to teens, but held a 'consciousness … emphatically adult' (p. 236).
9. In *10 Things I Hate About You* the song 'Cruel to be Kind' seems to illustrate this. It is a song written by Nick Lowe in the 1970s but is performed in the film by the contemporary band Letters to Cleo. However, the credits fail to acknowledge its original source.
10. Johanna Wyn and Rob White, *Rethinking Youth* (London: Sage, 1997), pp. 20–1.
11. Michael Brake, *Comparative Youth Culture: the sociology of youth cultures and youth subcultures in America, Britain and Canada* (London and New York: Routledge, 1985); Jenny Garber and Angela McRobbie, 'Girls and Subcultures: an Exploration', in Stuart Hall and Tony Jefferson (eds), *Resistance Through Rituals: youth subcultures in post-war Britain* (London: Hutchinson, 1976).
12. Henry Giroux, 'Doing cultural studies: youth and the challenge of pedagogy', *Harvard Educational Review*, vol. 64, no. 3 (1994), pp. 278–308 as quoted in Wyn and White, *Rethinking Youth*, p. 20.
13. Doherty, *Teenagers and Teenpics*, p. 237.

14. Jon Lewis, *The Road to Romance and Ruin: teen films and youth culture* (New York and London: Routledge, 1992), p. 64.
15. Tania Modleski, 'The terror of pleasure: the contemporary horror film and postmodern theory', in Tania Modleski (ed.), *Studies in Entertainment* (Bloomington and Indianapolis: Indiana University Press, 1986), p. 163.
16. E. Ann Kaplan, 'Feminism/Oedipus/postmodernism: The case of MTV', in E. Ann Kaplan (ed.), *Postmodernism and Its Discontents* (New York: Verso, 1988), p. 37. Referenced in Jon Lewis, *The Road to Romance and Ruin*, p. 98.
17. E. Sonnet, 'From *Emma* to *Clueless*: taste, pleasure and the scene of history', in D. Cartmell and I. Whelehan (eds), *Adaptations: from text to screen, screen to text* (London: Routledge, 1999), p. 59.
18. Wyn and White, *Rethinking Youth*, p. 66.
19. Brenda O. Daly, 'Laughing *with*, or laughing *at* the young adult romance', *English Journal* (October, 1989), p. 51. As cited by Lewis, *The Road to Romance and Ruin*, p. 69.
20. Jann Matlock, 'Reading dangerously: the memoirs of the Devil and Madame Lafarge', in her *Scenes of Seduction: prostitution, hysteria, and reading difference in nineteenth-century France* (New York: Columbia University Press, 1994).
21. Matlock, 'Reading dangerously', p. 279.
22. Ibid., p. 276.
23. Henry Jenkins, *Textual Poachers: television fans and participatory culture* (New York and London: Routledge, 1992), p. 167.
24. Notably, Julia Stiles who played Katarina Stratford in *10 Things* appears in both of the recent updates.
25. Thomas Cartelli, *Repositioning Shakespeare: national formations, postcolonial appropriations* (London: Routledge, 1999), p. 34.
26. Walter Benjamin, 'The work of art in the age of mechanical reproduction', in *Illuminations*, ed. Hannah Arendt, trans. Harry Zohn (London: Fontana Press, 1973), p. 215.

7

Peter Watkins's *Culloden* and the Alternative Form in Historical Filmmaking

Nicholas J. Cull

On the evening of Tuesday, 15 December 1964 British television audiences saw something remarkable. In the space of 71 minutes, a young director named Peter Watkins used all the news film techniques of the present to expose a wound of the past: the events surrounding the Battle of Culloden of 1746. By recreating the last battle to be fought on British soil and the brutal suppression of the Highland Scots that followed, Watkins reminded his viewers of the violence that had united the United Kingdom. He also struck at one of the most cherished myths of Scottish history. The film demolished the reputation of Charles Stuart. 'Bonnie Prince Charlie' was the hero of ballads like the 'Skye Boat Song', 'Will Ye No Come Back Again' and 'Charlie is Me Darling' and the face that decorated untold millions of souvenir shortbread tins, but he emerged from Watkins's film as a vain and foolhardy man, utterly unworthy of the devotion of the Highlanders who died trying to restore his family to the throne. Watkins's work also had contemporary relevance. *Culloden* attacked militarism in general. Moreover, by avoiding the conventions of fiction film and costume drama, and drawing on the techniques of documentary Watkins made his material seem as fresh, immediate and contemporary as the latest news of atrocities from the Congo. Audiences and critics greeted *Culloden* with almost universal acclaim, but Watkins was unable to develop either his political agenda or his distinctive technique in subsequent films. In later years he would look back on *Culloden* as his only film to escape the crushing hand of industry, conservatism and self-censorship and reach its intended mass audience. *Culloden* was 'the one that got away'.

By the 1960s the Battle of Culloden had been the stuff of myth for a century and a half. By the early 1800s the attempt of the 'Young

Pretender' Charles Stuart to rally the Highland Clans and seize the English throne from the House of Hanover had lost its political edge. It had become a convenient source for romantic stories. Victorian Britain embraced Scotland in general, and Bonnie Prince Charlie in particular, as an expression of its romantic sensibility. The novels of Sir Walter Scott were the most widely read books of the period. North of the Border tales of lost heroes like Scott's Rob Roy offered a special national identity within the overarching identity of Britishness. South of the Border, Bonnie Prince Charlie and his gallant Highlanders became a noble enemy, symbolic of the bygone age; local equivalents of the noble savages of Rousseau led by a latter-day Hector. The kilt, so politically charged as to have been illegal in the aftermath of the rebellion of 1745, was now the leisure garment of choice for Queen Victoria and her family while toying with the Highland life at Balmoral.[1] In the United States tales of the lost cause of Bonnie Prince Charlie became a particular favourite of the slave-owning south, where gentlemen boasted of descent from men who had made the final charge at Culloden. After their own cause was lost in the Civil War, they paid tribute to the spirit of 'Old Scotland's Hills' with a clan of their own.[2]

In the twentieth century the story of Bonnie Prince Charlie and the spirit of 1745 found emotive expression in the new medium of film. The prime vehicles for the celebration of the lost cause of the Highlanders were the multiple screen adaptations of Robert Louis Stevenson's classic novel set during the rebellion, *Kidnapped*. This story was filmed twice in 1917; in 1938 by Twentieth Century Fox; in 1948 by Monogram; and in 1960 by Disney, who operated a British studio at the time. Disney had already drawn on Highland mythology with their 1953 treatment of the 1715 rebellion, *Rob Roy, the Highland Rogue*; they knew the value of costume adventure to a British market. In 1963 BBC television adapted *Kidnapped* as a serial for the 'tea time' slot on a Saturday evening. The specific story of the Young Pretender had also produced two British historical films. In 1923 Charles Calvert directed Ivor Novello and Gladys Cooper in *Bonnie Prince Charlie* for Gaumont British, and in 1948 Alexander Korda famously squandered a succession of directors and a small fortune making a disastrous Technicolor film of the same name, with David Niven in the title role and Margaret Leighton as Flora MacDonald.[3] Such films did not recount the story of the rebellion to ask questions about the past or the present. They used the past as an antidote to the present, a realm of rich costumes and quaint manners to distract and uplift the audience. Hence by 1964 the events around the Battle of Culloden were both part of the cosy mythology of the United Kingdom and bound up in a particularly apolitical (and even conservative) approach to filmmaking: the costume drama. To tell the story differently was to challenge both.

Peter Watkins was born in the western suburbs of London in 1935.[4] He enjoyed a privileged education at a Welsh public school and the Royal Academy of Dramatic Art, before beginning his national service in the British army in 1954. Watkins narrowly avoided serving in the vicious guerrilla war then being fought in Kenya to quash the Mau Mau rebellion, but time served in the barracks of the East Surrey Regiment was enough to colour all his later work.[5] Watkins's first forays in amateur film show a commitment to the themes that would dominate his professional career. All displayed an abhorrence of violence; all challenged some element of national or international mythmaking; all represented a challenge to the dominant media narratives of his time; and all used historical events as a lever to pry open assumptions in the present.

Watkins's first film, *The Web*, was a brief 8mm piece dealing with the Second World War; astonishingly for the time, its sympathetic protagonist was a German soldier and his killers were members of the French resistance. Graduating to 16mm he made two films challenging the myths of United States history: *Field of Red*, dealing with the Civil War, and *Dust Fever*, a revisionist Western. He also completed *Diary of an Unknown Soldier*, depicting life in the trenches during the First World War. Watkins's most significant film from this era questioned not only the dominant narrative but also the dominant methods of filmmaking. His 1961 film *The Forgotten Faces* recreated the Hungarian uprising of 1956 using the techniques of documentary rather than fiction film. The Soviet Union had crushed the uprising, but the United States had done little to aid the rebels. The story thus provided fertile material for a rejection of both Moscow and Washington, and marked Watkins's emerging opposition to the Cold War. Watkins re-staged scenes from the uprising on the back streets of Canterbury, concentrating on the faces of the ordinary people involved. The result was so convincing that Granada television declined to show the film for fear that it might undermine genuine news footage. As one executive put it, 'if we show a film like that, no one will believe our newsreels'.[6] Fortunately for Watkins others were at least prepared to accept *The Forgotten Faces* as an apprentice piece. On viewing the film Huw

Wheldon, the charismatic new head of Television Music and Documentaries at the BBC, invited Watkins to make the film of his choice for the Corporation. Watkins responded by proposing a drama-documentary about the effect of an atomic bomb dropping on a typical British town. When Wheldon expressed some doubts about the project, Watkins produced a copy of a recently published history of the Battle of Culloden by John Prebble. Holding the book in the air, he asked, 'Could I make a film about this instead?' Wheldon agreed and *Culloden* was the result.[7]

On receiving the commission Watkins lost no time in contacting Prebble. After an initial meeting at Prebble's home in Surrey, Watkins made good use of the historian, who was happy to check over Watkins's script. Watkins even pressed Prebble to accept a co-authorship of the script, but he declined in favour of a simple acknowledgement as historical adviser. Watkins's script for *Culloden* followed Prebble's account to a remarkable degree. Prebble's book provided both the structure (it focuses on the battle and its aftermath) and most of the detail of Watkins's version. Prebble was the source for the dialogue of participants in events such as Lord Elcho's stinging call as his Prince Charlie left the battlefield: 'Run, you cowardly Italian.' The narration also came from his text: 'all witnesses agreed that if grapeshot were the king of battles then the bayonet was the queen of weapons'.[8] The most obvious change of emphasis in the transition from one text to the other was the weight that Watkins gave to economic details. He spent much time establishing the feudal nature of the Highland clan system and how debt brought Charles Stuart's men to the fatal moor. He also included telling details from Prebble's account to establish the nature of life in the British Army. We are told, for example, that it would take an enlisted man many years to earn the price of the wig worn by a captain.

The only major character prominent in Prebble's account but omitted from Watkins's version of the battle is the young Major James Wolfe, who in later years would earn his own place in British national mythology as the conqueror of Quebec. Prebble, who had grown up in Canada, could not resist mention of the man celebrated in song in 'The Maple Leaf Forever', but Watkins was unwilling to digress into debunking a particular British hero. Bonnie Prince Charlie and the clan system on one side and the Duke of Cumberland and the British Army on the other provided sufficient targets.[9] Watkins also avoided any language linking the events following Culloden to Nazi war crimes. There is no equivalent to Prebble's observation that three Lowland Scottish officers serving with the English had 'earned reputations that would not have been out of place in a mess of the *Schutztaffeln*.'[10] Watkins generally allowed his audience to draw their own parallels from the events on the screen, although his use of phrases like 'the pacification of the Highlands' encouraged the viewer to draw parallels with the numerous counter-insurgency wars then being fought in places like Malaya, Algeria and South Vietnam.[11]

Watkins soon assembled a structure for his film. The first half dealt with the battle, and took aim at the folly of Bonnie Prince Charlie, a man whose military experience before the rebellion was, Watkins informs us, attendance at a siege at the age of twelve. The second half of the film dealt with the brutality of the British in slaughtering the wounded after the battle and then in suppressing the Highlanders during the months and years that followed. Watkins passed over some of the most brutal material in Prebble's account to produce a balanced adaptation. For example, Prebble notes the extreme violence of the British soldiers, who roasted Scots to death and offered a £5 reward for the severed head of any rebel, but he also recounts the grisly discovery of rotting British bodies in a rebel's water cistern.[12] Neither Watkins nor Prebble left any room for national myth, sentiment, or Skye Boat Songs in their account. There were no heroes on either side, only victims. Neither man found anything on which to build a Scottish national myth for Scots fought on both sides of the battle. It was a war of Catholic against Protestant, Highland against Lowland, and even relative against relative. Prebble and Watkins both noted that the Chisholm family furnished officers for both armies.

Watkins made two critical decisions at the outset of his project. The first was to maintain his usual practice and use a cast of amateurs for the film. Later publicity for the film stressed that these 140 people were as close to the original participants in the battle as possible, 'perhaps descendants from the battle'.[13] The Scots were recruited locally and the English soldiers were found south of the border. Bonnie Prince Charlie himself was an Anglo-French student from Mauritius, Olivier Espitalier-Noel, who had been recruited in June 1964 from the London French drama group *Cercle dramatique Français de Londres*, after Watkins contacted the group's president, Maurice Chevalier.[14] His second key decision was to film the reconstructed battle using the latest techniques of documentary filmmaking.

In order to create the appearance of actuality Watkins employed an experienced BBC cameraman, Dick Bush, and a hand-held 16mm Arriflex camera. The immediacy of these images was compounded by Watkins's use of interviews to camera, which allowed the characters in the film to address the audience directly. The technique had been used before. In the early 1950s the US Columbia Broadcasting System had made *You Are There*, a series of interviews-to-camera conducted by Walter Cronkite, presenting reconstructed historical events.[15] But in *Culloden* the historical narrative was not fixed in an authoritative and all-knowing present, but fluid and unfolding in front of the audience. The level of reconstruction and the intensity of the action were of a wholly different order. Realism dominated the *mise-en-scène*. Watkins dressed his characters as authentically as possible. The drawn and dirty faces of the Highlanders would make a particularly powerful impact on the audience. Some Highlanders spoke only in Gaelic. Of course the filmmaker's art was also in evidence. Watkins shot the Highlanders from a high angle so that they would seem small and overshadowed by events. In contrast, the British Red Coats – photographed from a low angle – seemed enormous as they marched relentlessly towards the moor.

The film had a complex structure, with multiple levels of narration. The whole production began and ended with titles and commentary which might be understood as Watkins's own, objective voice (he spoke the commentary himself). This voice is able to speak with historical perspective. Within the film it becomes historically situated. It speaks in the present tense, asks questions of the principal characters and comments on the action: 'This is grapeshot. This is what it does.' However, it is also made clear that the era created its own historical record – an actor playing the Georgian historian Andrew Henderson appears in front of the camera conducting a running commentary on the battle in exactly the manner of a BBC war correspondent. Although some critics found this structure confusing, it allowed the audience rather more room to question the portrayal of events than a single 'voice-of-God' narrator.[16]

In some ways Watkins's approach suggested that contemporary documentary film techniques could strip away historical myths in a way that costume drama, national history and hagiography had failed to do. But *Culloden* also opened questions about the documentary medium. As well as unmasking the reality behind the myths of the past, the film was also a lesson in how the myths of the future would be fabricated. The camera itself became a character in the action, addressed directly by characters in the piece and making viewers aware that they were watching a construction. The most powerful moment of this kind of filmmaking comes when the death of Walter Stapleton, commander of the Stuarts' Irish allies, is held on the screen in a freeze frame. For all the realism of *Culloden* this was more stylised than anything in Korda's *Bonnie Prince Charlie*.

By November 1964 the film was complete. Watkins wrote to John Prebble and thanked him for his contribution: 'without your book this film would probably never have been conceived'. Before transmission *Culloden* was screened to an invited audience in London, including Prebble. As he recalled, the film ended with complete silence. The audience was simply too stunned to applaud.[17]

Immediately after the broadcast of *Culloden* on 15 December, the BBC's Audience Research Department compiled their usual assessment of reactions to the programme. Ratings were relatively low at an estimated 16 per cent, against 27 per cent of viewers watching Britain's other channel, ITV. Yet the programme had dramatic impact on those who had seen it. A 'housewife' reported that the events depicted were 'still capable of making one's blood boil'. Viewers commented on the 'tremendous anti-war impact'; a female viewer said, 'Such utter cruelty reminds me of recent events in the Congo.' A sales representative commented that the programme 'shattered forever all "romantic" thoughts of Bonnie Prince Charlie'. The BBC summary noted that viewers felt the film to be 'a superb piece of documentary craftsmanship showing not only an exhaustive and meticulous basis of research but, by imagination and originality of approach, the transformation of facts into human horror and pathos'. Some viewers felt that the realistic treatment of events produced images that were too horrific to screen, and others, while appreciating the value of the film, felt that the subject was 'too distressing to warrant enthusiasm'. Delighted with the reaction, the BBC repeated *Culloden* on 31 January 1965.[18]

Critical reactions to *Culloden* covered much of the same ground as the BBC's sample audience. Critics paid particular attention to the visual power of the film and its value as historical revisionism. *The Times* praised Watkins's attempt to 'scour the legendary patina from the brutal facts'.[19] Writing in *The Listener*, Derwent May noted particularly the power of the faces selected by Watkins.[20] Many commented on the anti-war message of the piece. Adrian Mitchell in the *Sun*, spoke of the 'Congo-like brutality' of *Culloden* and went on to observe, 'It will take a lot more than one documentary to undermine the romantic notion of war which has been, often deliberately, built up over the centuries. But *Culloden* helps.'[21] Unlike the BBC's public interviewees, some critics raised political objections to the film. L. Marsland Gander of the conservative *Daily Telegraph*, who had initially concentrated only on the practical aspects of making the film, belatedly realised its wider political implications and on 21 December condemned it as 'a sickening overdose of brutal savagery'.[22] Speaking for Scotland, Robert Kemp mourned the violence done to the old image of the Highlands and Bonnie Prince Charlie, noting that 'Prince Charles was accorded no last vestige of charm. Without it, the Rising becomes unbelievable.'[23]

The other voice of criticism came from an unusual quarter. The powerful British actors' union Equity objected to Watkins's use of amateur actors. Some months after the transmission of the film, Felix Aylmer, the president of Equity, declared to the press:

> The ragged highlanders looked wet, hungry and exhausted because in fact they were hungry and exhausted. He [Watkins] had kept them short of food and marched them on an empty stomach until the required degree of emaciation had been reached. Their falls when they were hit looked natural because they were natural. The army was driven through stretches of heather in which trip wires had been concealed.

Aylmer concluded that while this 'novel method of production' was new to Britain, it was familiar from ancient Rome.[24] The BBC legal department investigated the claim and established that there was no truth to the story.[25] However, the BBC resolved to appease Equity over its use of amateur actors. At a meeting with Equity in July 1965 the BBC defended their right to innovate in documentary but promised to consult Equity first before initiating another project along those lines. The BBC also discreetly sent the Equity actors' benevolent fund a cheque for over £1000, equivalent to the fees that would have been paid to a professional cast for *Culloden*.[26]

With the success of *Culloden* the BBC gave Watkins the chance to make *The War Game*, his film about the dropping of the atomic bomb. It was here that his problems began. The BBC declined to screen *The War Game* on the grounds that it would be too disturbing for the viewers, although the film did win an Academy Award for best documentary in 1966. As an Oscar-winner Watkins was then able to develop his fictionalised documentary style in such feature films as *Privilege* (UK, 1966), a satire on the British media; *Gladiators* (Sweden, 1968), an anti-war science-fiction piece; and *Punishment Park* (USA, 1970), which depicted a US penal system of the near future. Frustrations still abounded. *Punishment Park* was withdrawn from circulation in the United States after only four days. Watkins hoped that his anti-Bomb message might get onto German television. In 1968 Sudwest Funk of Baden-Baden commissioned him to make a film about what would happen if an atomic bomb hit Hamburg. They changed their minds and tore up the contract days before research began.[27]

Watkins responded to these setbacks by attempting to kick-start a debate on the media within Britain. In 1968 and 1970 he circulated two open letters to senior figures in British television pleading for social responsibility in British broadcasting. In a letter of 20 December 1968, received by the Director-General Charles Curran and the political journalist Robin Day amongst others, Watkins condemned the BBC insularity and its drift to the political right. In a wider letter of 9 March 1970 he compared Britain to the decaying Confederate South. He also attacked the new trends in Hollywood filmmaking and the unholy alliance between mass capitalism and the counter-culture that he saw in films like Arthur Penn's *Bonnie and Clyde* (1967).[28] Their exploitation of history and violence for cheap commercial gain flew in the face of everything that Watkins held dear. He returned repeatedly to the need for serious content rather than just entertainment. Watkins insisted that 'the public *is* concerned about life and its problems sufficiently to want marginally more than *Lucille Ball* and *Steptoe and Son* on television and *Carry on Dentist* in the cinema'. Determined to lead by example, Watkins returned to historical filmmaking. This time his subjects would be drawn from American history.[29]

Surrounded by news of race riots in American cities and atrocities in the Vietnam War, Watkins felt that America might profitably reconsider its past. As with *Culloden* he planned to assault both a mythic subject and the way in which that story was usually told. He planned a *Culloden*-style treatment of the genocide of the Plains Indians. Hollywood was not impressed. Watkins's first film project, a revision of the Custer legend called *Proper in the Circumstances*, was killed by Universal Studios after 14 months of research on the grounds that it was 'too documentary' in style and 'the general public knows all there is to know about General Custer'. His plan for an epic on the March of Death inflicted on the Cherokee by the Western 'hero' Kit Carson, *The Long March*, foundered in 1973 when a studio boss informed him: 'I don't care if Marlon Brando is in the film, no one will pay a cent to see it if you have interviews to camera.'[30] A trilogy of films on the American history – *The State of the Union* (dealing with the American Revolution, the Civil War and the destruction of the Nez Perce Indians) – also foundered. Even the National Film Board of Canada recoiled from Watkins. By his account they backed out of a project to make a film about the rebellions in the Canadian West of the 1860s and 1880s led by Louis Riel, muttering that Peter Watkins was 'a dangerous man'.[31] With the British equally unwilling to allow Watkins to make a film about the Irish Easter Rising of 1916, Watkins moved to Scandinavia.

In Scandinavia Watkins was able to make films that challenged the dominant mode of production in both the form and content. His work included *Munch* (Norway, 1974), a major work on the Swedish peace movement, *The Journey* (Sweden, 1983–86) and a film/video project dealing with August Strindberg, *The Free Thinker* (Sweden, 1993). As far as the British film establishment was concerned he was 'professionally dead'. His name was omitted from the British Film Institute's 1985 *History of World Cinema*.[32]

Despite Watkins's professional difficulties, *Culloden* continued to prosper, becoming one of the BBC's 'best sellers' in international distribution. In 1969 the film premiered in the United States. It was read, out of its original British context, as specifically critical of United States policy in Vietnam.[33] Such a reading denied the general anti-war message of the film and more seriously deflected attention from the implications of the film for British history and identity. In fact by concentrating on an interpretation on the Vietnam War from which the British wisely remained aloof, the critics ran the risk of affirming notions of British integrity and moral superiority that Watkins's film was intended to question. French critics had a clearer notion of *Culloden*'s purpose. Fernand Dufour greeted the film's French television premiere in 1974 by proclaiming the work 'subversive cinema'.[34]

In 1972 and 1976 the BBC re-screened *Culloden* as part of special seasons celebrating 50 years of the BBC in 1972, and 40 years of television transmissions in 1976. *Culloden*'s innovative attempt to question old British myths had, ironically, been appropriated by an emerging mythology of British excellence, the triumphalist narrative of British public service broadcasting. In 1972, smarting from being 'virtually completely black-listed from working in my own country', Watkins wrote to the Director-General complaining that the showing of *Culloden* 'reveals a lack of sensitivity and hypocrisy that is almost unbelievable'.[35] The 1976 re-showing sparked a more wistful response. With the disappointments mounting, Watkins noted that it had 'proved extremely hard to make this kind of film again'. He explained to Nancy Banks-Smith of the *Guardian* that:

> I found reluctance to look boldly and without fear at one's national history. I don't mean the prestigious kind of history, like Henry VIII, I don't mean that at all, but the intimacy and pain and compassion and passion of people who lived as we live now. There seems to be a fear of opening up one's own history in America and England ... *Culloden* got away with it and stands as an indictment of what can be done.[36]

A third of a century on from *Culloden*, there are few films that can be cited to dispute Watkins's claim.

Culloden lives on in the memory of historians and industry professionals.[37] Visitors to the Royal Armouries museum in Leeds are treated to clips of the film, but it has no living memorial in the contemporary presentation of history on film or television. The costume drama (sometimes mixed with the *Bonnie and Clyde*-style sexual twists or violence so abhorred by Watkins) continues to reign supreme. Although historical feature filmmakers are willing to examine the dark underside of modern history – including the Nazi genocide of European Jews and slavery in the Americas – they remain shy of experimenting with or interrogating form. Watkins has always questioned whether it is possible to rethink the past within a commercial medium that is embedded in present-day values. Responding to the acclaim for *Holocaust* and *Roots*, Watkins argued that the 'monoform' of the Hollywood family saga or blockbuster brought 'serious topics down to the level of mass entertainment'. '*Roots*', he noted, used 'the same rhythms as *Kojak* and *Love Story*'.[38] As the century drew to a close Watkins finally had the chance to apply his *Culloden* approach – including the techniques of contemporary reportage – to a new subject, the Paris Commune of 1871. The resulting film, *La Commune*, premiered in Paris in March 2000. The release was limited and the scheduling of the television broadcast of the film in the middle of the night did little to help the film. The coincidence of theme, form and supportive context that had gone to make *Culloden* such a success seemed unrepeatable.[39]

In 1996 Watkins left his new home in Vilnius, Lithuania, and returned to Scotland for a reunion with the amateur actors who had worked with him on *Culloden*.[40] So much of what he had attempted to do in the intervening years had been frustrated or belittled. There was a sad circularity in his return to the site of his first victory. Peter Watkins had laid bare the lost cause of Bonnie Prince Charlie only to become an exile himself and to see his alternative approach to historical filmmaking transformed into a creative 'lost cause'. Yet, as John Prebble remarked on the closing page of his book of 1961, 'A lost cause will always win a last victory in men's imaginations.'

Notes

1. On the Victorian cult of Scottishness, see Angus Calder, *Revolting Culture: notes from the Scottish republic* (London: I.B. Tauris, 1994).
2. The Southern myth around Bonnie Prince Charlie is discussed in W.J. Cash, *The Mind of the South* (New York: Vintage, 1991); the allusion is made at the moment of the foundation of the KKK in D.W. Griffith's *The Birth of a Nation* (1915).
3. The film cost Korda £550,000 but made only £250,000 during its domestic release. See Sue Harper, *Picturing the Past: the rise and fall of the British costume film* (London: British Film Institute, 1994), pp. 170–3, 217. Watkins's budget for *Culloden* was £3665; see BBC Written Archives Centre, Caversham Park (hereafter BBC WAC), T32/515/3, Revised budget, 31 March 1964.
4. The biographic details are drawn from Joseph A. Gomez, *Peter Watkins* (Boston, Mass.: Twayne Publishers, 1979), James Welsh, *Peter Watkins: a guide to references and resources* (Boston, Mass.: G.K. Hall & Co., 1986), pp. 1–25 and biographical notes by and on Peter Watkins, clippings collection, BFI, London.
5. Gomez, *Watkins*, p. 19.
6. Milton Shulman, *The Ravenous Eye* (London: Coronet, 1975), pp. 242–3.
7. John Prebble, *Culloden* (London: Secker & Warburg, 1961). The circumstances of the film were recalled by Prebble in a telephone conversation with author, 11 September 1997.

8. Ibid., pp. 106, 114. Prebble also put Watkins in touch with Colonel Iain Cameron Taylor of the National Trust for Scotland, who contributed much advice, see BBC WAC, T32/1, 164/1, general correspondence.

9. Ibid., pp. 20, 122.

10. Ibid., pp. 164, 218 and dust jacket of first edition.

11. For a survey of British counter-insurgency in this era see Susan L. Carruthers, *Winning Hearts and Minds: British governments, the media and colonial counter-insurgency, 1955–1960* (Leicester: Leicester University Press, 1995).

12. Prebble, *Culloden*, pp. 137, 189, 203.

13. This claim is reported (sceptically) in Richard Sear, 'A battle where the amateurs stole the show', *Daily Mirror*, 16 December 1964.

14. BBC WAC, T32/1, 161/1, Casting file: Bonnie Prince Charlie.

15. The similarity was noted by Peter Purser, *Daily Telegraph*, 16 December 1964. For a discussion of the difference between the two, see Gomez, *Peter Watkins*, p. 36.

16. Earlier that same year the BBC's *Tonight* unit had made good use of Michael Redgrave as a voice-of-God in their path-breaking 26-episode compilation documentary *The Great War*.

17. BBC WAC, T32/515/2, Watkins to Prebble, 17 November 1964 and interview John Prebble.

18. BBC WAC, T32/515/3, Audience Research Report, *Culloden*, 8 January 1965. The 'audience reaction index', a guide used by the BBC to compare different programmes, was high, at 67.

19. *The Times*, 16 December 1964.

20. Derwent May, 'Television of the month', *The Listener*, 21 December 1964.

21. Adrian Mitchell, *Sun*, 16 December 1964.

22. L. Marsland Gander, *Daily Telegraph*, 16 December and 21 December 1964.

23. Robert Kemp, 'Wae's me for BBC's Culloden', *Glasgow Herald*, 16 December 1964.

24. *Daily Express*, 25 April 1965 also *Sun*, 25 April 1965.

25. BBC WAC, R101/70/1, Management file: *Culloden*, C.J. Curran to legal adviser, 17 May 1966.

26. BBC WAC, T32/515/1, Meeting with Equity, 19 July 1965; T32/1, 163/1, Wadsworth (Contracts) to Souse (General Manager, Radio and Television), 25 August 1971.

27. Peter Watkins, Press Statement, July 1982, British Film Institute press clippings collection, London.
28. BBC WAC, R78/1, 987/1. In his letter of 9 March 1970 Watkins condemned what he called the 'Gangster-and-his-moll-slow-motion-machine-gunned-balletic-thunderspots-of-blood-son-of-motor-bike-rider-free-wheeling-pot-smoking-sun-flaring-into-lens-young-Revolutionary-generation-backed-up-against-a-wall-(blonde with jutting breasts, of course)-syndrome'.
29. BBC WAC, R78/1, 987/1.
30. Peter Watkins, Press Statement, July 1982, British Film Institute press clippings collection, London.
31. Ibid.
32. Peter Watkins, 'A statement by Peter Watkins, film maker and media teacher, regarding *The Free Thinker* and the crisis in mass audio-visual media and media education'. 1994, British Film Institute Pamphlet Collection (pamphlet 659.3), London.
33. Bonnie E. Williams, '*Culloden*', in *Film Library Quarterly*, vol. 2, no. 2, Spring 1969, pp. 15–16. Williams accepts this reading but defends *Culloden* as 'a great film', which although 'anti-war' was nonetheless 'pro-humanity'. On *Culloden*'s best-seller status, see BBC WAC, T32/1, 163/1, General Manager Television (Souse) to Head of Programme Contracts, 19 August 1971.
34. Fernand Dufour, 'La bataille de Culloden', *Cinéma*, 74, no. 187, May 1974, pp. 20–22.
35. BBC WAC, R78/1, 987/1, Watkins to Director-General, 27 November 1971; 9 January 1972 and associated correspondence.
36. Nancy Banks-Smith, *Guardian*, 28 August 1976. Watkins's reference to Henry VIII refers to the BBC's spectacular *The Six Wives of Henry VIII*, which had won critical acclaim in the early 1970s, and helped to cement the corporation's enduring attachment to costume drama.
37. Watkins's *Culloden* was singled out for praise in the plenary address of Christine Whittaker, 'History of BBC History' to the XVIIIth International Association of Media History conference 'Television and History', Leeds, UK, 14–17 July 1999 and by Steve Badsey at a one-day conference on the BBC's *Great War* series (1964), Queen Mary and Westfield College, London, 4 July 2000.

38. Scott MacDonald, *A Critical Cinema – 2: interviews with independent film makers* (Berkeley: University of California Press, 1992), p. 407.

39. On *La Commune*, see Peter Lennon, 'Hate and war', *Guardian*, 25 February 2000 and John Cook and Patrick Murphy, *Peter Watkins* (Manchester: Manchester University Press, 2001).

40. Interview: John Prebble.

8

Mrs Brown's Mourning and Mr King's Madness: Royal Crisis on Screen

Kara McKechnie

It is rather appropriate that grandfather and granddaughter should be respectively the subjects of *The Madness of King George* (Nicholas Hytner, 1994)[1] and *Mrs Brown* (John Madden, 1997), because the films are themselves related in their treatment of history, their accurate period detail, and, not least, in their parallels with the present. These two 'biopics' depict monarchs a century apart but much closer in their presentation on screen. This chapter focuses on the question of how history is presented on screen through an exploration of *King George* and *Mrs Brown* within the tradition of history films with monarchic themes. Both films seem prepared to sacrifice complete historical veracity in order to produce a film that has an appeal beyond an historically knowledgeable audience. Set in 1788 and in the 1860s respectively, both *King George* and *Mrs Brown* show strong connections with the time in which they were made – the 1990s with their real-life Royal drama. It is one of the aims of this chapter to look at the way in which the period of production influences the presentation of history on screen in the films.

The Madness of King George is Alan Bennett's adaptation of his stage play *The Madness of George III* (1991). First released in America in December 1994 (four months before it came to British cinemas), it won a wide audience and four Academy Award nominations.[2] Bennett had been known to a selected American audience since he had appeared in *Beyond the Fringe* on Broadway in the 1960s, but with *King George* he 'cracked' the American market. The film meets the American audience's cultural and visual expectations of the type of British history film, which has filled a 'niche' in the American market since the 1930s. To be profitable in America, British filmmakers are expected to produce texts in which the representation of the national past conforms, at least in part, to stereotypical ideas about a 'heritage' denied to American citizens by the youthfulness of their country. This notion of 'heritage' is often biased towards images of upper-class life because the concept is implicitly associated with displays of wealth and grand style. Pictorial treatments are often in a painterly style that complements a more theatrical approach to acting technique than is usual in Hollywood movies.

Joseph O'Mealy has described the changes that took place in converting Bennett's play from stage to screen.[3] Apart from the generic changes brought about by the screen adaptation, Bennett and the director, Nicholas Hytner, made choices that were clearly influenced by American market forces, such as the alteration of the title from *The Madness of George III* to *The Madness of King George*. This was a 'marketing decision', Bennett explains. Had 'George III' remained in the title, viewers would have come out of the film wishing they had seen the first two in the series as well.[4] Extravagant and stately in its display of locations, the film mirrors the frantic pace of the King's illness, and mixes the comic with the tragic. Its effect is to paint a differentiated portrait of a monarch whom public opinion tends to associate only with first losing the colonies and later his mind.

Briskness is not exactly the defining element of *Mrs Brown*, made from an original screenplay by Jeremy Brock. Like *King George*, it owes a lot to the tradition of the monarchy film and has distinctive – especially visual – heritage film characteristics. The film was made on a low budget – a mere £1m – and partly financed, like *King George*, by Channel 4. Director John Madden later made a leap from the relatively conventional stylistics of *Mrs Brown* to the more complex and experimental *Shakespeare in Love* (1998), a spectacularly self-referential and intertextual history film with a budget of £25 million. *Mrs Brown* is an 'actorly' film, starring Judi Dench and Billy Connolly, with other distinguished players like Geoffrey Palmer and Anthony Sher in the cast. The film's success both at home and overseas was partly due to its release around the time of the Princess of Wales's funeral, which influenced its reception more than the marketing campaign.[5] It was then believed that Princess Diana was hunted to death by paparazzi,[6] employed to satisfy the public's constant appetite for gossip and scandal. Ensuing national mourning and guilt caused the nation to restrain this appetite and to be sympathetic towards the Royal pursuit of personal happiness, which is the theme of *Mrs Brown*. It makes use of the historical uncertainty over the relationship of the Queen and her favourite servant, John

Brown in a 'tasteful' way, not portraying any consummation, but constantly hinting at the possibility and inviting speculation. The affair was a destabilising factor for the Royal Family: after her reclusive and intense period of mourning in the early 1860s, the Queen stayed out of public life for several more years, and was accused of being out of touch with her people, mocked in *Punch*[7] and nicknamed 'Mrs Brown'. Her absence provoked calls for disestablishing the monarchy and her unwillingness to 'give him up to them'[8] was perceived as disloyalty and lack of interest in her people in the 1860s.

Because they both deal with historical themes, the two films have been lazily lumped into the critically suspect category of the 'heritage film'[9], a classification developed in the 1980s, largely to denigrate texts that seemed to share an affinity with Thatcherite views of the national past and which avoided ideological engagement with the present. The association of 'heritage' with 'reactionary' has discouraged serious critical engagement and allowed the films to be dismissed as visually indulgent but artistically uninteresting. Rather than immediately assigning *King George* and *Mrs Brown* to this dismissive category,[10] it is more useful to examine their relationship to the wider genre of history film, and the sub-genre of the Royal biopic, before assessing their heritage credentials.

Monarchs in History

The history film has been an intermittent feature of British film production and its appearance often coincides with times of constitutional crisis. Films such as *Victoria the Great* (Herbert Wilcox, 1937) and *Sixty Glorious Years* (Herbert Wilcox, 1938) were produced after the Abdication Crisis of 1936, one of their intentions being to restore the public's confidence in the stability of the monarchy.[11] Stability, however, is not a dominant theme of *King George* and *Mrs Brown* and this fact alone says much for the changed face of monarchy films in the last decade. The films depict both George III and Queen Victoria as troubled, incapable of mustering 'the strength to be who [they] must be',[12] not filling their monarchic role and therefore destabilising the state. This royal 'vacuum' is caused by mental and physical illness in *King George* and by Victoria's paralysing grief in the years after Prince Albert's death in *Mrs Brown*. Although inherently criticising the royal incapability, both films concentrate on showing the person rather than the monarch and evoke strong feelings of sympathy and compassion for both George III and Queen Victoria.

Sue Harper gives a detailed account on the early days of the history film and also demonstrates how many difficulties are posed by attempting a precise categorisation. Very generally, one can distinguish between the history film, which, although not a blueprint for historical accuracy, is concerned with actual historical figures and the costume film, which is set in a recognisable historical period, but with fictional characters. Within the history film category there is a small but distinctive number of films about monarchs, the most famous being *The Private Life of Henry VIII* (Alexander Korda, 1935), *Victoria the Great, Sixty Glorious Years, Tudor Rose* (Robert Stevenson, 1936) and *Fire over England* (William K. Howard, 1936). These early history films were considered an ideal medium for propaganda and therefore often subject to official pressure. The Foreign Office substantially influenced the depiction of monarchs in history films like *Royal Cavalcade* (1935).[13] Robert Vansittart, Head of the Foreign Office since 1930, even co-wrote the script for *Sixty Glorious Years*. Nowadays there are no such demands on the filmmaker, enabling more varied and experimental choices in the representation of history.

Two of the most noteworthy director/producer-figures of the early age of these films, the 1930s, were Alexander Korda and Herbert Wilcox, who represented different approaches, but were not always consistent within the body of their own work. This applies especially to Wilcox, who appears to have been a producer 'with no firm views of his own'.[14] It was Korda's film *The Private Life of Henry VIII* that started the fashion of monarchy films in 1935. A big commercial success, it encouraged a steady number of royal biopics well into the postwar years. Harper suggests that Korda's commercial strategy was not only to 'foreground sexual pleasure' but also to deploy 'historical periods to exploit cultural resonances to the full' by presenting images of the national past with which British and overseas audiences were already familiar.[15]

It would be easy to say that all early monarchy films bear the characteristic of mythologising the figure of the monarch, but the great variety of debates about historical accuracy, profit-oriented producers and different directorial approaches makes this problematic.[16] While some films exploit and expand royal outrageousness, dragging the monarch down to earth, *Victoria the Great* celebrates the centenary of Queen Victoria's accession by almost canonising the Queen, balancing the need to keep her as human as possible at the same time. Wilcox was influenced by the upheaval of the crisis of 1936 in the planning stages of *Victoria the Great*.[17] The 64 years of Victoria's reign are a celebration of the monarchy's lasting endurance, which in 1937, one year after the abdication crisis, was an important measure to restore the public's confidence in their rulers. Naturally, the film can be read as a reassurance about the stability of the monarchy and the Victorian family. Given that Edward VIII was perceived as having given up his throne for love, both *Victoria the Great* and its follow-up, *Sixty Glorious Years* (1938), make the important point that royal duty and a happy married life can be combined. The film can also be seen as satisfying the audience's escapist notions for a time 'when things were better' in a period of high unemployment and political uncertainty. Though a not very pleasing and somewhat schematic film, *Victoria the Great* is a useful example of how films dealing with the past can link with the time in which they are made. This is also true of *Sixty Glorious Years*, an 'intimate diary' of the Royal couple's life together, made a year later by Wilcox with the same cast in the main parts.[18] Written with more literary ambition than *Victoria the Great* by Wilcox and Robert Vansittart, it contains a very clear endorsement of the contemporary politics of appeasement, especially with Germany. The Duke of Wellington remarks that it is 'the most important thing' to 'keep friendly with your neighbours'.

Though praised for their attention to visual detail, both films' representation of history is subject to pragmatic convenience and official influence and they are selective and sometimes biased about the historical facts. Firstly, public events of historical importance are reduced to captions and picturesque tableaux, acting merely as a backdrop for the portrayal of personal relationships. Secondly, Wilcox's urge for completeness allows only very short time to individual occurrences during Victoria's sixty-year reign. The drive to mythologise the figure of the monarch is remarkably different from *Mrs Brown* and in fact most of more contemporary history films: the two Victoria films aim to legitimate monarchical rule by stressing its role in bringing about social stability, prosperity and imperial glory, and to soothe the embarrassment of the abdication affair by depicting Royal marriage as the model of patriarchal family relationships.[19]

Wilcox's two Victoria films therefore have to balance the responsibilities of both lifting and controlling the public spirit in volatile times. If history films are indicators of stability, *Beau Brummell* (Curtis Bernhard, 1954) demonstrates the secure position of the monarchy in the year after Queen Elizabeth II's coronation. The fact that it is possible to parody her ancestors, George III (Robert Morley in full raging lunacy) and his son, George IV (Peter Ustinov as a spoilt and immature wimp) illustrates what liberties can be taken in times of stability.

In the 1960s and 1970s the critical representation of the monarchy became part of a more oppositional (or at least less reactionary) cinema, with history films such as *A Man for All Seasons* (Fred Zinnemann, 1966) and *The Charge of the Light Brigade* (Tony Richardson, 1968). Royal biopics were less plentiful, but when they did appear, they served as a vehicle for emerging issues, such as the rise of feminism. In *Mary Queen of Scots* (Charles Jarrott, 1972), for instance, Mary is sympathetically portrayed as a victimised yet strong woman who acts according to her heart, and Elizabeth as a shrewd monarch who has successfully adopted male ruling strategies. The film deals with the conflict experienced by women in traditionally patriarchal roles: 'That monarch [Mary] is first a woman ... this woman [Elizabeth] is first a monarch.'

During the 1980s the taste for historical subjects was principally satisfied by the kind of literary adaptations that provoked the heritage label, but the practice of demythologising monarchs on screen has had a revival in the mid-1990s. Just as *Victoria the Great* was influenced by the real royal drama that unfolded during its production, both *Mrs Brown* and *King George* responded to the crisis in the monarchy that reached boiling point in the 1990s. The monarchy was in the process of losing its function as a role model, and the absence of any elementary public crisis meant that there was no need to be reassured, as during wartime or after the abdication crisis in 1936. Instead, the public's appetite for gossip and insight into the royal family's private life revived the 'market' for royal biopics. With varying degrees of obviousness, films like *King George* or *Elizabeth* (Shekhar Khapur, 1998) index the real royal crisis unfolding in the House of Windsor through historical parallels. The ways in which past Princes of Wales have been represented offer examples: in *King George*, the later George IV is portrayed as idle and frustrated at being condemned to wait: 'But Pa, I want something to *do*.' – 'Do? Well, follow in my footsteps, that's what you should do.'[20] In *Mrs Brown*, the future Edward VII is kept firmly in check by his controlling mother, who has little faith in his competence. The two filmic portrayals deliberately mirror the predicament of the current Prince of Wales.

In recent years, there has been a change in the royal family's function as a 'model family': with the monarch's constitutional role nearly extinct, the family is reduced to a mere royal soap opera, where before it was a more elevated symbol of familial harmony and perfection. Even though *King George* ends with a royal tableau that seems to reinstate this perfection, it is undermined by the audience's knowledge that sanity is only restored for a short time. George III's instruction, 'We must be a model family for the nation to look to',[21] cannot be carried out in an age where smutty phone conversations are recorded for the delectation of the public, private letters are passed to the tabloids and the whole idea of the first family as a role model is deconstructed. Following the breakdown of the Prince and Princess of Wales's marriage, revelations about both parties' extra-marital affairs and psychological defects, and the almost symbolic fire at Windsor Castle, the Queen was reduced to declare 1992 an *'annus horribilis'* and to employ spin doctors for the reconstruction of the royal image. The real-life royal family's emergence as a dys-functional family unit quickly found its parallels in royal biopics on screen. Alan Bennett claims not to have followed the royal separation during the production process of *The Madness of George III* in 1991 or the subsequent film version in 1994,[22] but contempo-rary parallels are so thick on the ground that the possible influence of other royal issues can hardly be ignored.[23]

While public opinion of the first family was more favourable in the wake of Princess Diana's death in 1997, a recent poll suggests its popularity has dropped to an all-time low.[24] The filmic portraits within *King George* and *Mrs Brown* stress the tension between the flawless picture the nation is presented with and the private monarch in distress and turmoil, and the measure of restraint needed in daily life. Contrast this with films such as *Victoria the Great, Tudor Rose* and *Sixty Glorious Years*, which are not an investigation into the monarch's private life or revelations of illness and affairs but underline the model character and self-sacrificing nature of the monarch. In our psychologically enlightened age, it is not acceptable to present restraint as a virtue and *King George* and *Mrs Brown* act accordingly, showing the dark side of the constant struggle of seeming royal.

In *King George*, when the King seems totally unable to control his behaviour and is at the height of his crisis, a new doctor whose methods are decidedly untraditional is brought to Windsor. Dr Willis's approach to the King's alarmingly unrestrained behaviour is that he must be artificially restrained until he 'remembers how to behave himself'. Thus, hurling abuse and fighting his captors, the King is seized and strapped into a chair. The restraining chair serves as a metaphor for the royal condition within constitutional monarchy and parliamentary democracy, symbolising the control of regal power. This is manifested by the soundtrack from the instrumental beginning of the coronation hymn 'Zadok the Priest', when the King's limbs are fastened to the chair. The introduction builds up crescendo and pace, while he is lectured by Willis on why he is to be restrained. As the mouthpiece of the restraining apparatus, gagging the King, is fastened, the chorus simultaneously bursts out in fortissimo with the first line of the anthem. We are shown a perversion of a coronation, a de-crowning of a monarch stripped of his voice, his power, his sanity and his dignity, with the restraining chair as a caricature of the throne. When the King has recovered and is congratulated on being more himself, George III replies that he has always been himself, but has only now remembered how to *seem* himself.[25] Similar themes of royal restraint are to be found in *Mrs Brown*, although the psychological similes are much more subtle. To establish the theme, we are shown the Queen being dressed by her servants. The shot begins in close on the back of Victoria's head, moving away to reveal details of very tightly plaited hair, which is put into place and then restrained by a black bonnet. The maid tying the ribbon to keep the bonnet in place pulls it together too tightly, forcing a muted expression of pain from the Queen.

The shift from mythologising a monarch to revealing him/her, madness and all, is significant, but it is surprising how consistent the other characteristics of the history film have proved to be. The expectations of audiences, especially those in America, continue to ensure that British history films are differentiated from their Hollywood equivalents. Therefore little has changed since Alexander Korda remarked in 1933 that the more national characteristics these films had, the more general their appeal would be. [26]

From this discussion one might conclude that which we might identify as the 'postmodern' treatment of history – the tendency to be historically selective to meet audience expectations and filmmaking trends, and to use allegorical comment to confront different periods with each other in one film – has existed as long as monarchs have been portrayed on screen. History films of the 1990s generally differ from earlier productions in the *conscious* announcement of the need to be selective in order to meet the demands of drama; not feeling any need to apologise for inaccuracies, but exploiting them for the benefit of entertainment.

In conclusion, it appears that a comment in defence of Korda's *Henry VIII*, 'the muse of the cinema was the cap and bells rather than the cap and gown',[27] still holds true. Making history pleasingly entertaining has always come first in the genre that makes use of 'the pull of the past'.[28] As long as this past *looks* convincing, we will generally not question the facts we are presented with in the films; the films therefore capitalise on our widespread ignorance about history. As a contemporary reviewer of *The Private Life of Henry VIII* remarked, 'Of course it is an emotional and ignorant picture of the past, and it would never do for an honours school ... but we are most of us pretty ignorant, really, about the past.'[29]

Harmless History?

The debate on the heritage film shows two clear tendencies: one is to read the films as conservative works, creating an idealised past 'when everything was better', to compensate for limitations in the present; secondly, the critics invariably comment on the films' visual presentation of the period they are portraying. This refers to the importance the average heritage film will devote to the display of buildings, costumes and landscapes and to the way the camerawork relates to these displays. The tendency here is not so much to analyse the specific visual text or subtext of a film, but to comment on what this display means in the context of the genre. The opinion most commentators voice is that through its heightened importance and accuracy, the visual overshadows the meaning of the historical narrative. Moya Luckett, for example, takes this position, arguing that while films can have a stylish look, their historical content is often shallow and modified to fit marketing strategies.[30]

In allowing the viewer to escape into the past with the help of pleasing, idealised visual evocations, heritage films have been accused of providing not much more than a distraction and purely augmenting the British tourist industry's income. The following argument addresses itself to the criticism that heritage films serve as 'conservative escapism' and encourage historical 'dumbing down' by placing too much emphasis on the visual. Escaping into an historical past requires a certain interest and even competence.

Engaging with the past in any form, especially in a context that pays great attention to how the past *looked*, can be beneficial. Historical awareness is not just conveyed through words; one may argue that to get an instinctive sense of the period may be seen as more valuable than knowing the chronological details of its public events. History teachers often introduce a period through music, slides of contemporary portraits and sound recordings of witnesses before building the 'factual' information on the 'impressionist' foundation. In this light, it is somewhat shortsighted to blame American audiences for the historical simplifications of period films. They are simply part of an audience that collectively suffers from selective knowledge, often concerning a period that is out of personal reach and therefore somewhat abstract. While it is understood that the viewers' (sometimes deplorable) lack of accurate knowledge is taken advantage of and marketability can dominate 'factual' history, the simplifications can also be understood as measures to make the relevant history more accessible. It is therefore difficult to see why the films' historicity should be annulled by an emphasis on the visual. The pictorial simply constitutes *another* kind of historicity, which happens to be on a non-verbal level. Labelling films as 'heritage' can therefore lead to reductionism in their reading.[31] What audiences make of the relationship between the visual and the narrative aspects of history films remains an open question.

Examples from *King George* and *Mrs Brown* usefully underline the cause of visual historicity: the King's state of mind finds a visual equivalent in the presentation of Windsor Castle (or rather Arundel Castle doubling for it):

> There should be a sense too that what happens to the King in the course of his illness is reflected in the topography of the castle. His behaviour, previously geared up to the public and state rooms, gradually becomes inappropriate for such settings; when he periodically escapes into the back parts of the castle ... it's comparable to his escape into the back parts of his personality.[32]

The phases of the royal disease are illustrated by the colours dominating the respective shots: the clear royal colours, blues, reds and purples open the film, but become too bright and irritating, as illness sets in. When the situation becomes more desperate, the colours take on a more melancholic quality, muted shades of blue and grey, lit like a period painting. Colour is practically reduced to black and white when the King, still deteriorating, is 'banished' to Kew Palace for the winter. The use of a soft-focus lens in some of the mad scenes mirrors the King's fading eyesight (he went completely blind in 1811). As spring sets in and the monarch starts to recover, the colours take on an optimistic touch, the sunlight not too bright and unsettling as before, but warm and soothing. With the King's temporary recovery, the clear shades of royal blue and red optimistically dominate the screen once more.

The camerawork in *Mrs Brown* manages to capture the odd-couple status of the outsider John Brown and the Queen by constructing impeccably symmetrical images and then breaking them up. With difficulty, the Queen has been convinced that she must interrupt her rigid mourning regime and go riding with Brown. The scene begins on the balcony shot from behind the shoulders of two identically dressed footmen positioned between two identical columns. As the camera slowly moves down to a symmetrically arranged pathway, we see Brown, leading his pony with the Queen riding it, walking away from this rigid arrangement. The picture is a harmonious one, but future problems caused by difference in rank are hinted at by their difference in height, created by the Queen's elevated position on horseback. Lengthy establishing shots, like this one, starting with the camera lovingly gliding over built heritage, do not exclude the possibility of a psychological reading and can provide a powerful subtext to a film.

Undoubtedly, history films (and their heritage subgenre) like *King George* and *Mrs Brown* work to please their target audience, and this audience is generally not to be found amongst the worshippers of cutting-edge avant-garde. Both films serve their audience's need for memorable tableaux, but also work on two other levels: educational, because they give the viewer the possibility to develop a sensual/instinctive awareness of the era; and psychological, because the visual subtext is a psychologically coded system of its own. History films of this kind can open a door to a period too far removed for us to have any personal knowledge of it, by conjuring up a sense memory through visual imagery. The denial that the films have any concern with 'serious' history is part of a debate about the ideological function of heritage films.

Critics often deem heritage films conservative, because they can be seen to serve as a 'social emollient' which offers a 'profoundly conservative' vision of the past.[33] The argument generally side-steps the issue of whether films present history in an inaccurate way but concentrates on the films nullifying the subversion of the narrative (in this case the work they are adapted from, mostly novels).[34] This is partly due to the fact that there can always only be *versions* of history, however closely the film is based on 'facts'. Films like *Shakespeare in Love* and *Gladiator* (Ridley Scott, 2000) pepper their historical subjects with modern references, although they have to keep postmodernism on a narrative rather than a visual level. Filmmakers like Ridley Scott recognise that the conscious evocation of period through production design is essential to the suspension of a spectator's disbelief.[35] *Plunkett and Macleane* (Jake Scott, 1999) also supplies this visual accuracy, while offering a full postmodern historicity, laced with modern anachronisms, such as a soundtrack that mixes techno with period liturgical music.

Which Generation?

Displaying a high degree of accurate period visualisation, *King George* is not as comfortable with the way it displays history as are later films in the genre. Alan Bennett is notorious for always being in two minds about everything. In the case of *King George*, this expresses itself in wanting to stay true to his roots as an historian, but also wanting a successful film; not wanting to 'sell out' to Hollywood demands, but not wanting to be confined to the less seductive narrative that sticking to the confirmed facts invariably offers. Ironicising his contradictory position, Bennett 'would like this film to be a masterpiece, if it can be arranged'.[36] Like Bennett, the film comes across as not having committed itself, firing literary references, contemporary parallels, comedy and tragedy elements at the audience, while still trying to maintain its historical credentials. This breadth of ambition distinguishes *King George* from most 1980s heritage films, and it also differs from them in pace and focus. Where they maintain a leisurely tempo, *King George* has a constant drive; where they focus on a love story, the relationship between the King and his wife is just one of many themes, and the affair between Lady Pembroke and the equerry Greville is too minor to support the film's plot structure.

Crucially, however, the film distances itself from the heritage genre in its approach to history. Heritage films are often described as escapist, transporting the viewer into an idealised period in the past. Despite beautiful locations, the depiction of a mad King who is neither able to control his words nor his bowel movements does not make for this kind of escapism and neither does an original text full of historical *double entendres* that quite aggressively draws parallels with the present.[37] Unlike the typical heritage film, which is an adaptation of a classic novel, *King George* is the adaptation of a stage play and this has strong implications for its pace, again distancing it from its 1980s heritage 'ancestors'. It is much more in accordance with earlier history films like *The Private Life of Henry VIII*[38] and points in the direction of history films produced later in the decade. *King George* displays some anachronisms which could be read as postmodern, but Bennett is not really of a postmodern disposition, expressing concerns about taking liberties with historical facts. And so, under the medium's merciless rule, the Prince of Wales has to take on the part of the villain, more than is suggested in historical records, and has to be cast as better looking and slimmer than his stage version.[39] The King's recovery is given dramatic impetus by bringing the King to Parliament *just* in time to prevent the passing of the Regency Bill, although history books tell us this personal appearance did not take place.

Prefaces have always been Bennett's safety net; they are as much an introduction to what is *not* included as they are to the contents and background of the play/script. Bennett, in anticipation of dumbing-down criticism, justifies the film's different emphasis with the text's transition from stage to screen. In the introduction to *King George* we see that Bennett, while understanding the need for departures from 'fact', is still far from being playful with history:

> 'No time' is, of course, always the problem. Film is drama at its most impatient ... There's a bit more leeway on stage, depending on the kind of story one's telling, and more still on television, where the viewers are so close to the characters as not to mind whether they dawdle a bit. But with film, meandering is out of the question; it has to be brisk, so most of my atmospheric backstairs stuff never made it to the final film – so little, in fact, that I wonder now how I could ever have thought it would, and was that preamble to the script just a sales pitch.[40]

Jeremy Brock, the scriptwriter of *Mrs Brown*, is more at ease with his mission, acknowledging that detailed research makes it difficult to distinguish between 'what you invent and what you remember'.

This might have worried me had I been writing a history piece but I wasn't, I was writing about love ... everything else, including historical accuracy, would have to be subordinated to the demands of the narrative. Obviously, much of what happens in the film is well documented and there is still a recognisable chronology, but far more important to me is that the spirit of the piece should be true. To an historian this may sound like heresy, but even the strictest biographies are, by definition, subjective and in the end, we all guess.[41]

Brock's attitude makes it easier to make the vital decisions that determine a film's success and make it homogeneous. Paradoxically, he is of a more progressive disposition than Bennett, but *Mrs Brown* is not necessarily more progressive than *King George* as a result. Its more settled pace and its dominant theme, a love story, may be one of the reasons why *Mrs Brown* comes across as a film that has greater coherence than *King George*. It also has clearer heritage-credentials, if the term is not used pejoratively: although not an adaptation of a novel, as most heritage films are, its pace, its camerawork and especially its visuality make *Mrs Brown* as much a continuation of the likes of *Howards End* as it is of the royal biopic.

King George and *Mrs Brown* are descendants of a long lineage of history films. Their 'ancestors', from the 1930s onwards, have been subject to fashions, which are largely determined by contemporary events and their resulting national moods. This applies especially to monarchy films, where the contemporary degree of royal stability will often determine how the monarch in the film is depicted. It seems that if there is a need for reassurance, monarchs will be mythologised, just as they will be made all too human in times of stability. Certainly *King George* and *Mrs Brown* conform to this pattern and are therefore first and foremost a continuation of the royal biopic. Royal crises of the 1990s influenced the genre's revival and show it in transition, moving away from the 1980s heritage ideology and towards a postmodern aesthetic.

The very fact that the films are concerned with monarchy tends to make them conservative in the eyes of critics, because their creation is automatically assumed to be a statement in favour of the monarchy. The assumption is partly correct for *King George* and *Mrs Brown*. Although critical of George III and Queen Victoria's destabilising of the state, both films never seriously invite the opinion that there should be constitutional changes as a consequence.

Change is always shown as a distinct possibility, but not supported by the 'message' of the films. The monarchic rule is presented as the natural state and the viewer's sympathies are clearly drawn to the troubled monarch. However, we feel compassion for the *person* rather than the ruler. It is a sense of tradition rather than of active royalism that makes us uncritical of the constitutional implications of our sympathy for the monarch. The films' positions are therefore more socially reactionary than politically conservative. Bennett explains that he certainly has no political reasons for having 'royalist inclinations': 'I'd just like to be able to take it for granted as one used to do. I don't want to have to think about it. I just want it to be *there.*'[42] The statement is indicative of his anxiety about change and his emotional affinity with the past, a condition quite common in the British history film itself.

Notes

1. Hereafter referred to as *King George*.
2. Nominations: Best Actor: Nigel Hawthorne; Best Supporting Actress: Helen Mirren; Best Writing, Screenplay based on material from another medium: Alan Bennett; Best Art Direction – Set Decoration: Ken Adam, Carolyn Scott (won).
3. 'Royal Family Values: The Americanisation of Alan Bennett's *The Madness of George III*', in: *Film and Literature Quarterly*, 5 (1998), pp. 90–6.
4. Alan Bennett, *The Madness of King George* (Screenplay) (London: Faber & Faber, 1995), p. xiii.
5. Like *King George*, *Mrs Brown* was first released in the US (18 July 1997) and then in the UK (5 September 1997), but it was particularly American reviewers who compared Queen Victoria's and Princess Diana's dilemmas: 'The inescapable image is of Diana striding into the new century with a coltish grace that left the Royal family rooted in the past. She showed Britain the same spirit that John Brown sought to instil in Victoria. This graceful, witty movie now assumes an awful sadness.' Review by Joan Ellis, Nebadoon, <http://ellis.nebadoon.com/docs/ joined_reviewfiles/MRS_BROWN.html>.
6. '...a girl given the name of the ancient goddess of hunting was, in the end, the most hunted person of the modern age.' The Earl Spencer's funeral address to the Princess of

Wales, Westminster Abbey, 6 September 1997, <http://www.etoile.co.uk/Royal.htm>.

7. A satirical Court Circular published in *Punch* is mentioned in the film: 'On Tuesday, Mr John Brown enjoyed a display of sheep-dipping by local farmers.' Jeremy Brock, *Mrs Brown* (Screenplay) (London: Methuen, 1997), pp. 41f.

8. Brock, *Mrs Brown*, p. 47.

9. The name 'Heritage Film' was given to a group of films, most of which were made by Ismael Merchant and James Ivory in the 1980s. Well-known examples are *Room with a View*, *Howards End*, *The Remains of the Day* (all Merchant Ivory, 1985, 1991 and 1993) and *The Wings of the Dove* (Iain Softley, 1997). There is no room here to include a detailed description of their characteristics, but there is an interesting debate, the exponents of which are Andrew Higson and Claire Monk. John Hill (*British Cinema in the 1980s* (Oxford: Oxford UP, 2000)) offers the best summary of their views.

10. Pamela Church Gibson, for example, calls *Mrs Brown* a 'more conventional Heritage offering'. 'Fewer weddings and more funerals: changes in the heritage film', in Robert Murphy (ed.), *British Cinema of the 90s* (London: BFI, 2000), p. 123.

11. See also Sue Harper, *Picturing the Past* (London: BFI, 1994), p. 53.

12. Brock, *Mrs Brown*, p. 56.

13. '[The Foreign Office] attempted, often successfully, to intervene in film production, distribution and publicity, and it gave priority to the issue of history.' Harper, *Picturing the Past*, p. 15.

14. Harper, *Picturing the Past*, p. 184.

15. Ibid., p. 29.

16. Sue Harper points out tendencies: in the period 1933–35, history films tended to be politically liberal and sexually permissive (films such as *The Private Life of Henry VIII* and *Nell Gwynn* (Herbert Wilcox, 1934); reacting to that, between 1935 and 1937, history was portrayed as a warning and had conservative tendencies (films include *Victoria the Great* and *Tudor Rose*), with the end of the 1930s seeing an emphasis on visual pleasure and again becoming more liberal (films include *The Four Feathers* and *The Return of the Scarlet Pimpernel*). *Picturing the Past*, pp. 186–7.

17. See also Harper, *Picturing the Past*, p. 53.

18. Anna Neagle plays the Queen across the ages (Harper blames Wilcox's 'uxorious devotion' to Neagle for some serious casting

errors); Anton Walbrook, everyone's favourite German, takes the role of Prince Albert and even the part of John Brown is played by the same actor (Gordon MacLeod) in both films.

19. In *Victoria the Great*, the Queen is shown to rule relying heavily on Albert's advice, who is the one who rules at home. There is a famous scene where the Royal couple has a power struggle over whether the Prince Consort should be allowed to smoke a pipe. He angrily withdraws and Victoria, knocking on the door, can only appease him by reducing his questions of 'Who's there?' from 'The Queen', 'Victoria' to 'Your wife, Albert!'

20. Bennett, *King George*, p. 74.

21. Ibid.

22. Ibid., p. xvi.

23. Bennett remembers that 'there was certainly a lot of rewriting going on'. He also recalls Prince Charles coming to a performance and neither of them mentioning the rather obvious parallels between himself and the Prince of Wales in the play. Platform on *The Madness of George III*, Royal National Theatre, 14 November 1999.

24. See, for example, the *Guardian*'s polls on 12 June 2000: 27 per cent of those questioned thought the nation would be better off without the royal family, 29 per cent are indifferent and only 44 per cent are in favour.

25. Bennett, *King George*, p. 65.

26. Harper, *Picturing the Past*, p. 20.

27. Ibid., p. 23.

28. Geoff Brown in Murphy (ed.), *British Cinema of the 90s*, p. 33.

29. Harper, *Picturing the Past*, p. 23.

30. In Murphy (ed.), *British Cinema of the 90s*, p. 88.

31. 'A particular consequence of this reductionism was that the early-1990s critiques allowed no space for the ambiguity and polysemy of heritage film texts', Claire Monk, 'The heritage film and gendered spectatorship', *Close Up: the electronic journal of British cinema*, <http://www.shu.ac.uk/services/lc/closeup/monk.htm>.

32. Bennett, *King George*, p. vii.

33. Robert Hewison, *The Heritage Industry* (London: Methuen, 1987), p. 47.

34. Pamela Church Gibson, in Murphy (ed.), *British Cinema of the 90s*, p. 116, on the filmic version of *Howards End*: 'This palpable

pleasure in parading the visual splendour of the past undermines the social criticism of Forster's novel.'

35. *The Making of* Gladiator, ITV, 4 May 2000.

36. Bennett, *King George*, p. vii.

37. 'There are some fortuitous parallels with contemporary politics; and had the play been written before the downfall of Mrs Thatcher there would have been more.' Alan Bennett, *The Madness of George III* (London: Faber & Faber, 1995), p. xvii.

38. Bennett knows Korda's films and remarks that 'With Pitt, I had first to rid myself of the picture I retained of him from childhood when I saw Korda's wartime propaganda film *The Young Mr Pitt*', *The Madness of George III*, Introduction, p. xv.

39. When Alan Bennett gave a guest lecture at Brighton Pavilion, he felt obliged to apologise to the staff of the site (famously created by the Prince Regent, later George IV) for his portrayal of the Prince of Wales in the film. I was told this by a guide at the Royal Pavilion. Rupert Everett, cast as the Prince of Wales, is not fat, like Michael Fitzgerald, who took the part in the first production of *The Madness of George III*, Royal National Theatre, 1991.

40. Bennett, *The Madness of George III*, pp. vi f.

41. Brock, *Mrs Brown*, p. vi.

42. Bennett, *King George*, p. xvi.

9

The Grandfathers' War: Re-imagining World War I in British Novels and Films of the 1990s

Barbara Korte

The war of 1914–18 raised the issue of memory even while still in progress. War neurosis was often associated with amnesia (treated literarily as early as Rebecca West's *The Return of the Soldier*, 1918), and its psychological treatment, as practised in Britain by William Rivers, consisted in recalling traumatic experiences. Conversely, after the war many former combatants were haunted by their memories and, after a period of silence, were at last able to communicate them, as the wave of war memoirs and novels around the late 1920s testifies. But the war of 1914–18 is not only a matter of personal recollection. As an ur-catastrophe of the twentieth century, it has also become a major facet of collective or cultural memory – at least in some cultures.[1] In Britain, World War I has indeed become a 'myth' of modern culture, as Paul Fussell, Samuel Hynes and many others have pointed out in seminal and well-known studies.[2] Here the 'Great War' has been kept alive in collective memory, through acts of public commemoration,[3] exhibitions, TV documentaries and the arts until today. In fact, as the end of the twentieth century was approaching, interest in the war became particularly strong again, especially after 1989, in the face of a major reorganisation of Europe. A decade that set in with the Gulf War looked back to the Great War in documentaries such as the BBC's *1914–18: The Great War and the Shaping of the Twentieth Century* (1997/98) and *The Western Front* (1999, in co-production with the History Channel), a major exhibition at the Imperial War Museum ('The First World War', 1998) and novels such as Pat Barker's *Regeneration* trilogy (*Regeneration*, 1991; *The Eye in the Door*, 1993; *The Ghost Road*, 1995) and *Another World* (1998), Sebastian Faulks's *Birdsong* (1997), Robert Edric's *In Desolate Heaven* (1997) or David Hartnett's *Brother to*

Dragons (1998). Major feature films included the adaptation of Barker's *Regeneration* (1997) and *The Trench* (1999).

Asking whether there are features peculiar to this decade's retrovisions of World War I, this chapter will concentrate on fictional examples, since it is here that the process of meaning construction, the *creative* moment in all acts of (personal and cultural) remembering, is foregrounded. As David Lowenthal writes in *The Past Is a Foreign Country*: '[t]he prime function of memory ... is not to preserve the past but to adapt it so as to enrich and manipulate the present'.[4] Despite the fact that it has been heavily mythologised, World War I has never been preserved as a static, unalterable myth: 1914–18 has always been a site of memory under construction and reconstruction, as can be observed by looking at the way it has been represented in the decades preceding the 1990s. The culture-critical 1960s, for instance, de-accentuated the 'great' war's patriotic values in the new context of a sceptical national self-examination and emphasised the suffering and pity associated with the soldiers' experience to convey a strong anti-war message. Characteristically, it was in this decade that the poems of Owen and Sassoon became canonised school texts used by teachers 'who had been involved in the Campaign for Nuclear Disarmament and later in the anti-war campaigns concerning US involvement in Vietnam'.[5] Works of art originating in the 1960s, like Joan Littlewood's *Oh! What a Lovely War* and Benjamin Britten's *War Requiem*, imagined the war in conformity with the prevailing climate.[6]

The new view found influential and popular scholarly expression in the work of Arthur Marwick, among others, whose *The Explosion of British Society 1914–62* (1963) and *The Deluge: British Society and the First World War* (1967) were popularised through their paperback editions and became set texts at higher education level. Marwick's interpretation of the Great War as a final release of explosive forces that had troubled British society for some time and would change it forever – namely, the rise of the working class and women's emancipation – has meanwhile become part of the war myth itself, with considerable influence on recent imaginative literature about that war. The rediscovery of the war's significance for women and the roles women played in 1914–18 was predictably intensified in the context of 1970s feminism, alongside a new interest in other 'counter-experiences' of the male combatants, such as those of conscientious objectors and mutineers.[7] Such interests were pursued into the 1980s, but the 80s retrovision of the Great War[8] also took place within the neo-conservative climate under Thatcher, which – especially around the Falklands War – gave rise to a new cultural discourse and a vehement counter-discourse about patriotism, nationalism and British or English cultural heritage in general. Retrovisions of 1914–18 in the 1990s are affected not only by their own particular present, but also by the heritage of myth and revision outlined above.

Across a gap of generations, writers and filmmakers in the second half of the twentieth century have had to rely on historical sources about the war[9] and what has sedimented in collective memory as war images or myths through documentary evidence (especially photography and documentary film), well-known scholarly work,[10] but also and to a considerable extent through earlier literature as well as other art forms. Many of today's sedimented images of the Great War go back to the canonised painting and poetry of the war itself and (some of) the war literature published about a decade after its end which, according to Hynes, gave the myth of the war 'its fullest definition'.[11]

Thanks to their standing in the school syllabus, the war poets are the most popular 'image' and 'experience' source for a wider twenty-first century audience. This may explain why Barker's *Regeneration*, which features Owen and Sassoon as shellshocked patients of Rivers in Craiglockhart Hospital, not only won critical acclaim but also reached a considerable readership, although it is technically more demanding than Faulks's more middlebrow *Birdsong*. Significantly, the film adapted from *Regeneration*, with its more restricted story and populist approach, focuses even more poignantly on the two poets and their relationship, especially their collaboration on 'Anthem for Doomed Youth', certainly *the* classic of World War I poetry. In contrast to the novel, Owen's role is also strengthened; he is the first character we see after the titles. He is also the last, since the film, departing from the novel, shows us what happens to Sassoon and Owen after they have left Craiglockhart Hospital: Sassoon is injured in the head (accidentally shot by one of his own men), and Owen lies dead in the water of the Sambre-Oise canal – tragically and ironically after we have already seen short scenes of the German surrender and the celebration of Armistice at Craiglockhart. It then also becomes obvious that earlier images of this canal in the film (for instance while we hear Owen read 'Anthem') are not pictures in Owen's memory but images foreshadowing his death. The film's final scene shows Rivers reading about Owen's death in a letter he has received from Sassoon, who encloses one of Owen's final poems. The poem is read in Owen's voice, over a close-up of Rivers who is moved to tears.

The myth of the Great War popular since the 1960s, the senseless slaughter of young men that calls for (Owenesque) pity, is thus more pronounced in the film than in the original novel. This is also obvious at the film's very beginning before the titles. It opens with a bird's-eye view of dead and injured men in a heavily mudded trench system. Since this shot cannot be ascribed to any character but is an external view, it is suggested that we are approaching this scenario from the shared vantage point of cultural memory. The next scene, after the titles, shows Owen, haunted by his war memories, walking through a forest where he finds an even more severely traumatised patient whom he prevents from committing suicide. The film is, like the novel, set primarily in Craiglockhart Hospital and uses flashbacks into battle action sparingly. Those war images shown are however, again, the standard ones – ruined landscapes, mutilated men – and they are drenched of colour. This effect certainly helps to distinguish the flashbacks from the present in Craiglockhart. But it also makes these flashbacks look like the familiar black-and-white war photography and cinematography and thus suggests a distanced historical quality – which their war memories certainly do *not* have for the traumatised patients in the action.

The other major British Great War film of the 1990s, *The Trench*, presents little more than the standard, 'mythic' experience of the trenches. Set entirely in a trench on the eve of the Battle of the Somme, it depicts an infantry platoon and their reactions to the experience they are about to face. Several reviewers noted that the film looked familiar; for instance David Horspool in the *TLS*, who also claimed that he had seen better versions of the myth:

> the actors look far too healthy and fit to convince as the under-nourished faces which stare back from contemporary photographs. The trench itself looks somehow too snug and well-tended, with only one of Sassoon's rats in evidence; even the latrine would impress a visitor to a modern-day campsite. Another problem is that the war has been written about and filmed so often that it is difficult to avoid stereotypes. The under-age volunteer, tough sergeant, boastful cockney and nervous junior officer might once have been credible, but we have seen them before.[12]

Where war films convey an impression of *déja vu*, novels evoke a similar sense of *déja lu*. In British literature, the prominent site of war memory is the Western Front,[13] and the war action in the 1990s novels, whether highbrow or middlebrow, also takes place in the trenches of Flanders and the Somme, with their standard associations of mud, vermin and 'burned and blasted trees'.[14] There is the stock action element of going over the top at the officers' whistle, and the resultant carnage in no man's land. Shellshock and mutilated bodies are depicted in ghastly detail. Disfigurement of the face as the mirror of a person's identity and 'soul' is depicted in several novels as a particularly tragic form of physical mutilation.[15] 'Familiar' themes and motifs further include parallels between the soldiers' martyrdom and Christ's Passion (especially through Cross imagery[16]), or related biblical stories of suffering, like that of Job in Hartnett's *Brother to Dragons*, which derives its title from Job 30:29–30. A predictably prominent biblical allusion is also still frequently made to the Apocalypse; it is found conspicuously and systematically in Hartnett's novel. The dragon in the novel's title not only comes from a verse in the Book of Job, it also refers to Satan in Revelation 12:9, when Satan is hurled to the earth, to lead the whole world astray. Another familiar element in many recent war novels is the idea of two worlds – that of an idyllically perceived prewar society shattered by the war and an utterly antithetical postwar world.[17] We find the comradeship of the men at the front (with or without homoerotic undertones) as well as the soldiers' disillusionment about the purpose of the war, their distrust and even hatred of civilians,[18] or the uncommunicability of their combat experience to those who have not shared it.[19]

The 1990s novels and films also continue and elaborate some of the re-visions of the war that have become familiar since the 1960s. Besides giving detailed accounts of physical and mental martyrdom (the latter often in direct-consciousness passages that used to be rare in the immediate postwar treatments of shellshock), some novels render the experience of pacifists and conscientious objectors – a prominent theme, for instance, in Barker's *The Eye in the Door*. Emphasis is likewise laid on the class and gender aspects of the war experience. Like novels and films of the preceding three decades, 1990s fictions narrate the experience of ranks other than officers, whose perception dominated the memoirs and novels of the immediate postwar decades. Lower-class characters are now frequently focalisers of the action, as Jack Firebrace in *Birdsong*, Billy

Prior in the *Regeneration* trilogy, or the limeburner Eric in *Brother to Dragons*. The class issue is particularly foregrounded in the latter novel. It is class – besides personal – antagonism that brings the two male protagonists to the Western Front. Charles Tremain is the son of the family that owns the quarry in which Eric works. When the intense love-hate relationship between the two men culminates in a tug-o'-war contest that Eric wins, Charles has to accompany Eric to the front although he has always been a coward. His revenge is to remind Eric of their class difference that will also mark their soldier's life: 'But remember ... you'll be my servant. I'll have a commission. So no nonsense. And remember to salute an officer at all times' (p. 170).

In Barker's trilogy, it is Prior who betrays such a marked class con-sciousness. He repeatedly and openly reflects about his position as an officer promoted from the ranks and how his view of the war thus differs from that of members of higher levels of society. Prior is also the main character through whom Barker pursues the relationship between the war and the definition of gender and sexual roles. Prior falls in love with Sarah, a munitionette (that is, a working-class woman's role in the war rarely literarised before), but also has an affair with an upper-class former officer in *The Eye in the Door*. Homo-eroticism is one of the myths associated with the Great War already found in the classic memoirs. According to Fussell, this homoeroti-cism was often a 'sublimated (i.e., "chaste") form of temporary homosexuality. Of the active, unsublimated kind there was very little at the front'.[20] Read against this genteel version of the myth, Barker's treatment in the trilogy is unsublimated and, in some of the language used to address the theme, seems late rather than early twentieth-century: for instance, when Prior, supervising his men bathe (another stock element of the literary front), thinks that the '[w]hole bloody Western Front's a wanker's paradise' (*The Ghost Road*, p. 532).

The criticism of a certain anachronism has been pronounced against Barker's general treatment of the gender issue.[21] When Prior first meets Sarah in *Regeneration*, his view on the war's effect on women is tinged by a later feminist interpretation:

> He didn't know what to make of her, but then he was out of touch with women. They seemed to have changed so much during the war, to have expanded in all kinds of ways, whereas men over the same period had shrunk into a smaller and smaller space. (pp. 82f)

Similarly, in *The Eye in the Door* the daughter of an imprisoned female pacifist talks to Prior about meeting a former suffragette friend:

> And she was ... *full of herself.* Short hair, breeches, driving an ambulance, all things she'd never've been allowed to do in a million years. And suddenly she grabbed hold of me and she said, 'Hettie, for women, this is the first day in the history of the world.' (p. 297)

In particular, Barker's presentation of Rivers's views on the re-definition of masculinity as a factor of war neurosis seems strongly inspired by Elaine Showalter's *The Female Malady* (1987), one of Barker's acknowledged sources:

> In leading his patients to understand that breakdown was nothing to be ashamed of ... that tears were an acceptable and helpful part of grieving, he was setting himself against the whole tenor of their upbringing. They'd been trained to identify emotional repression as the essence of manliness. Men who broke down, or cried, or admitted to feeling fear, were sissies, weaklings, failures. Not *men.* (*Regeneration*, p. 44)

Interestingly, in her later novel, *Another World*, Barker herself addresses anachronism as a problem inherent in later generations' visions of the war. A female historian of the 1990s, who interviews a war veteran, tries to impose her views on the interviewee and meets with astonished incomprehension: 'She tried to get Geordie to frame his war experience in terms of late-twentieth-century preoccupa-tions. Gender. Definitions of masculinity. Homoeroticism. Homo-*what*? asked Geordie.' (p. 83)

However, that the gender issue and the question of women's roles in the war is a prominent late-twentieth-century concern is obvious in other novels as well – not only those written by women, like Helen Dunmore's *Zennor in Darkness* (1993), where the central character is a young woman who experiences the war years in her native Cornwall. In David Hartnett's *Brother to Dragons*, a major part of the action is focalised through Beatrice, a young teacher who later becomes a VAD (Voluntary Aid Detachment) nurse because this is closest she can get to the front experience of the two men to whom she feels fatally bound. Another female character in this novel,

Maud, is a former suffragette who works as a munitionette and whose language occasionally seems as out of period as the passages criticised in Barker's novel: 'Fucking. That's all they're good for. Men, I mean. Fucking. Don't forget that, Beatty. The only thing a man can do better than a woman is piss into the wind' (p. 202). Hartnett also makes a great effort to imply that not only men suffer in the war, not even hesitating to make Beatrice's extremely painful menstruation an image of female 'martyrdom' during the war. Similarly, Robert Edric's *In Desolate Heaven*, a novel set in the immediate postwar years and emphasising the suffering of the survivors, portrays not only male war invalids but also women who cannot overcome the pain of having lost their loved ones. One character, Mary, develops an extreme eating disorder – another physical condition particularly associated with women – and tries to starve herself to death. Even *Birdsong*, despite its pronounced focus on the male trench experience, introduces a female sufferer; Stephen's former French lover, Isabelle, is maimed in the face when her house is hit by a shell.

The most prominent theme, however, to give the 1990s novels their distinguishing mark, is a preoccupation with how the war can be remembered at all – not only from the point of view of participants in that war, but from that of later generations. Writers here fictionalise their own problems in looking back to and re-presenting a war remote from their own lived experience. They also embed their war fictions in the generally intensified interest – scholarly and literary – that phenomena of memory have received over the last few decades.[22]

The novels use different techniques to address the problem of retrospection that World War I poses to the later-born. The strategy employed by Hartnett is a form of hypermythopoeia that presupposes how the war has already been mythologised and which lays this process of mythmaking bare by taking it to extremes. Significantly, *Brother to Dragons* begins with an epic opening that sets the action in a time that seems long past: 'In those days ...' (p. 3). Also, in a number of passages, a truly omniscient narrator comments on the action from a superior awareness of the events' outcome and consequences. What happens in the quarry in the summer before the war breaks out is seen as inevitably leading to the battlefields:

> Those who were left could see how, from the depths of Lower Pit, invisible ribbons began, tracing a path that led for many to the low chalk slopes of the Somme. The defeat of the quarrymen [in

a tug o' war] was their entry, premature, unlooked for, into a world
of war. (p. 55)

Allusions to myth, whether religious or secular, pervade the entire
novel, such as the suffering of Job and the dragon symbolism
mentioned above. The strongest mythical force, however, is
generated within the fictional world itself: an apocalyptic myth
which the quarry community has constructed around their ancient
hill. A dragon is believed to dwell deep under that hill; one day it
will be woken up, the hill will explode, and the quarry will be
destroyed in a deluge. The antagonism of Charles and Eric makes the
myth come true. The hill, which has been unstable for some time
(one could hear a rumble from its depths), is destroyed by an
explosion and a subsequent flood devastates the entire area. The
expected catastrophe turns out to be, at the same time, the
'explosion' of the war (an idea possibly derived from Arthur
Marwick), and the ancient quarry thus becomes emblematic of a
prewar world in which explosive social force has accumulated: 'For
generations now the pits and their ever-spreading slum in Quarry
Bottom had been a source of conflict and difficulty: labour disputes,
standoffs, even the odd riot' (p. 6). The connection between this
explosive potential and the ensuing war is indicated on the novel's
symbolic level: the thunder of the Battle of the Somme later to be
heard across the Channel sounds exactly like the rumble that could
be heard from the hill (p. 322). The quarry is also already trenchlike,
through the quarrymen's work, but also through the archaeological
digs conducted there by the representatives of the upper class, out of
a patriotic interest in English prehistory that is explicitly linked to
the patriotism used to legitimise the war: 'That is how old our civilisation is, that is how far we reach back. Now isn't that something
to be proud of, to fight for, all those generations that have gone
before us, in this beautiful place?'(p. 158).[23] The link between the
war and the condition of England is developed further when Charles,
shellshocked and in panic, does not return to the front after home-
leave and (in reversal of Brooke's foreign field that is for ever England
in 'The Soldier'), literally transforms Beatrice's garden, 'her little plot
of English earth' (p. 383), into a trench system. The signification of
this episode is quite obvious and in line with the Great War myth:
England will be changed forever by the war; it will never be a
pastoral garden again. By hypermythologising the war, Hartnett

suggests, quite in Fussell's tenor, that the war has become a myth and, for later generations, is only accessible *as* a myth.

Other novels address the problem of retrovision quite differently, establishing a meta-memorial level to articulate explicitly the difficulties which later generations have in remembering and re-imagining World War I. Faulks's *Birdsong* attempts this through a separate storyline that interrupts the novel's wartime action.[24] This memory plot is set in the year 1978, when the granddaughter of the war protagonist, Elizabeth, gets interested in her grandfather's experience. This effort of recovery is triggered by newspaper reports on the occasion of the sixtieth anniversary of the Armistice, but also by a personal consideration. Wondering whether she should remain childless or give birth to a member of a new generation, Elizabeth gets interested in the 'lost' generation of World War I and what they were fighting for. 'Because their lives were over she felt protective; she felt almost maternal towards them' (pp. 266f). For Elizabeth, the war thus suddenly gains significance, stops being 'ancient history' (p. 257). She then uses many of the resources through which her generation can still approach the war: she visits the battlefields on the continent and is overwhelmed by their testimony of slaughter, especially by the mass of names on the Thiepval memorial. She also speaks to the few surviving veterans from her grandfather's regiment, who cannot tell her much any more. Only when she finds her grandfather's war notebooks does she feel 'close' to the authentic war experience. For the reader of *Birdsong*, however, this notebook is already a processed experience, since the reader, thanks to fictionalisation, has the privilege of direct access to the grandfather's war experience.

Faulks's memory plot strikes one as rather straightforward (as does the entire novel) when compared to Pat Barker's *Another World*. This text addresses the generational differences in Great War memory without the device of a separate memory plot, but with greater complexity than *Birdsong*. The novel's single plot line takes place in the 1990s: the problem of remembering the war is embodied in a literal sense, through Geordie, the grandfather of the novel's male protagonist Nick. Geordie, aged 101 and dying of cancer (although he believes that his pain is caused by a bayonet wound), is haunted by his memories of the war and actually relives his war experiences. In particular, he is haunted by the fact that he killed his brother Harry on the battlefield – believing that he was mortally injured, but perhaps, as he now suspects, out of hatred and jealousy. Although

Geordie's memory of all other war experiences is extremely acute, his memory fails him in this crucial respect, causing a trauma which he carries to his grave.

Where Geordie has problems remembering a single war event that he has experienced himself, his middle-aged grandson has the problem of sharing Geordie's memories. Nick has grown up with a grandfather who, for many years, could not communicate his war experiences at all. Only in the 1960s did Geordie discover his duty, as one of the war's last eye-witnesses, to talk about it to young generations, for instance at one of the prime sites of collective war memory in Britain, the Imperial War Museum: 'His message was simple: *It happened once, therefore it can happen again. Take care*' (p. 82). Geordie has also talked to a historian, Helen, the character through whom a meta-memorial dimension is explicitly introduced into this novel. Her research is devoted to how one person's memories change over time because they are affected by 'the changing public perception of the war' (p. 81):

> Helen was interested in the reasons for these changes, in the social forces that had obliged the young Geordie to repress his memories of fear, pain, bitterness, degradation, because what he had thought and felt at that time was not acceptable. A later generation, fresh from a visit to *Oh! What a Lovely War*, the 'Dies Irae' of Britten's *War Requiem* pounding in its ears, couldn't get enough of fear, pain, etc. The horror, the horror. Give us more. Suddenly a large part of Geordie's experience was 'acceptable', though still not all. (pp. 82f)

How Helen tries to get Geordie to 'frame his war experience in terms of late twentieth-century preoccupations' (p. 83), especially gender-related ones, has been mentioned above. Nick, much as he likes Helen, feels that this late-twentieth-century approach is a distortion of his grandfather's memories: 'For Helen, memories are infinitely malleable, but not for Geordie. Geordie's past isn't over. It isn't even the past' (p. 241). He tries to empathise with his grandfather, accompanies him on a last visit to the battlefields and war cemeteries. Here Nick, like the granddaughter in Faulks's novel, is overwhelmed by the sheer number of deaths, especially at Thiepval.

> If, as Nick believed, you should go to the past, looking not for messages or warnings, but simply to be humbled by the weight of

human experience that has preceded the brief flicker of your own few days, then Thiepval succeeded brilliantly. (p. 73)

Apart from this (meta-)dimension of remembering World War I, *Another World* also addresses the impact of the past on the present in wider terms, through a Gothic subplot involving Nick's postmodern composite family. He and his wife have three children, two from their respective earlier marriages, and a toddler they have in common. They have moved into a Victorian house that seems to be haunted by a family tragedy of its previous owners who made their fortune as arms manufacturers in the Great War. Nick finds out that the elder siblings of that family murdered their little stepbrother – an incident that is almost repeated in the present. Nick's family is troubled by ghosts of the past just as Geordie is by World War I and especially the idea that he might have killed his brother.

It is in such a widening of concerns beyond the immediate war experience that some fictions of the 1990s go beyond earlier ones. Others, like Dunmore's *Zennor in Darkness*, modify the 'familiar' retrovision by focusing on less mythologised aspects of the war, or they choose little-worn settings, like the Swiss spa in Edric's *In Desolate Heaven*. No matter how far they extend and modify the matter of the Great War, however, all novels and films discussed still re-imagine the war in terms of sedimented images and thus help to perpetuate a certain cultural memory. But at the same time, since cultural memory is continually under re/construction, at least the more challenging examples also help to reinvent that memory by adding perspectives of the late twentieth century.

Notes

1. In Germany, by contrast, the collective memory of 1914–18 has been superseded by the catastrophe of the Second World War and in particular the Holocaust. For a theoretical discussion of collective and cultural memory, see M. Halbwachs, *Collective Memory* (New York: Harper & Row, 1980), J. Le Goff, *Histoire et mémoire* (Paris: Gallimard, 1988) and P. Nora (ed.), *Les Lieux de mémoire* (Paris: Gallimard, 1984ff), as well as more recent ones such as P. Connerton, *How Societies Remember* (Cambridge: Cambridge University Press, 1989) and J. Fentress and C. Wickham, *Social Memory* (Oxford: Blackwell, 1992).

2. P. Fussell, *The Great War and Modern Memory* (Oxford: Oxford University Press, 1977 [first pub. 1975]); S. Hynes, *A War Imagined: the First World War and English culture* (London: Bodley Head, 1990).
3. This now even encompasses deserters. *The Times* of 15 March 2000 reports on the vote of a Kent village to officially commemorate the first British soldier to be shot for desertion in World War I (11).
4. (Cambridge: Cambridge University Press, 1985), p. 210.
5. S. Featherstone, *War Poetry: an introductory reader* (London: Routledge, 1995), p. 10.
6. C.M. Tylee, *The Great War and Women's Consciousness: images of militarism and womanhood in women's writings, 1914–64* (Iowa: University of Iowa Press, 1990), p. 2.
7. Tylee, *The Great War*, p. 16. As Hynes and Bracco (*Merchants of Hope: British middlebrow writers and the First World War, 1919–1939* (Oxford: Berg, 1993)) point out, cowards, conscientious objectors or working women *are* found in considerable numbers in the literature and other arts of the war years and the immediate postwar decades, but were then forgotten and did not become part of the war mythology. This applies especially to the literature written by women on their experience of the war – see M.R. Higonnet *et al.*, *Behind the Lines: gender and the two World Wars* (New Haven: Yale University Press, 1987), p. 13.
8. Relevant novels of this decade include J.L. Carr's *A Month in the Country* (1980), filmed in 1987, Paul Bailey's *Old Soldiers* (1980) or one of the historical plot strands in Graham Swift's *Waterland* (1983). Films and television treatments include the adaptation of *The Return of the Soldier* (1982), *How Many Miles to Babylon* (1982: a film adapted from the 1974 novel by Jennifer Johnston), *The Monocled Mutineer* (1986), a new version of R.C. Sherriff's *Journey's End* (1988), *Blackadder Goes Forth* (1989) and Derek Jarman's *War Requiem* (1988).
9. Pat Barker, for instance, acknowledges some of her non-fictional sources in the novels of the *Regeneration* trilogy. For *Another World*, the published edition does not mention any sources, although Fussell must have inspired a character's reflection about the war's standardised field postcard with its first sentence, 'I am quite well.' Fussell finds this sentence 'close to brilliant' in the way it 'allows one to admit to no state of health between being "quite" well, on the one hand, and, on the other,

being so sick that one is in hospital'. (*The Great War and Modern Memory*, p. 185). In the novel, a character is fascinated by 'that word "quite". Does it mean "fairly" or "absolutely"?' (*Another World* (Harmondsworth: Penguin Books, 1999), p. 230). (Subsequent page references are to this edition and are included in the text).

10. Such as Fussell, E.J. Leed, *No Man's Land: combat and identity in World War I* (Cambridge: Cambridge University Press, 1979) and recently Hynes and J. Winter, *Sites of Memory, Sites of Mourning: the Great War in European cultural history* (Cambridge: Cambridge University Press, 1995).

11. Hynes, *A War Imagined*, p. x.

12. 'Remember the Rats?', *Times Literary Supplement*, 1 October 1999, 19.

13. A rare exception is William Boyd's novel *An Ice-Cream War* (1982), with its setting in East Africa.

14. S. Faulks, *Birdsong* (London: Vintage, 1994), p. 133. Subsequent page references are to this edition and are included in the text.

15. See, for instance, *The Ghost Road* (P. Barker, *The Regeneration Trilogy* (Harmondsworth: Penguin 1998), p. 542 – subsequent references are to this edition and are included in the text) and *Birdsong* (p. 155) for two such scenes. Mutilated faces are also thematised in Hartnett's *Brother to Dragons* (London: Cape, 1998: subsequent references are to this edition and are in the text) and Edric's *In Desolate Heaven* (London: Anchor, 1998: subsequent references are to this edition and are in the text).

16. On crucifixion, see Fussell (*The Great War and Modern Memory*, p. 118). For references in 1990s novels see, among many other examples, *Birdsong* (p. 121), *In Desolate Heaven* (p. 51), *Regeneration* (p. 133). In the *Regeneration* film, one of the last trench scenes begins with a panoramic shot of a big cross on a hill. Resurrection is an element closely associated with the Christ parallel. Stephen in *Birdsong* twice raises from the dead (see p. 180 and the entire final episode), and after the battle on the Ancre the survivors rise 'like a resurrection in a cemetery twelve miles long' (p. 239). In Edric's *In Desolate Heaven*, resurrection seems only possible in the animal world when Hunter and Jameson remember birds apparently dead from shock of a starburst miraculously restored to life (p. 306).

17. As an element of the war myth, this motif is discussed by Bergonzi (*Heroes' Twilight: a study of the literature of the Great War* (London: Constable, 1965) p. 20), Fussell (*The Great War and*

Modern Memory, p. 80) and Hynes (*A War Imagined*, pp. ix–xi). In the 1990s novels, it is particularly prominent in Faulks's *Birdsong* and in *In Desolate Heaven*.

18. See Sassoon and Prior in Barker's *Regeneration* trilogy, Weir and Stephen in Faulks's *Birdsong*, or Jameson in Edric's *In Desolate Heaven*.

19. This is discussed as a typical war experience by Fussell, *The Great War and Modern Memory*, pp. 169f. For relevant passages from novels of the 1990s, see, for example, *Birdsong* (pp. 141, 150) and *In Desolate Heaven* (p. 309), where the central female character reproaches Hunter for being unable to speak about his trench experiences.

20. Fussell, *The Great War and Modern Memory*, p. 272.

21. See Löschnigg, '"... the novelist's responsibility to the past": History, Myth and the Narratives of Crisis in Pat Barker's *Regeneration* Trilogy (1991–1995)', *Zeitschrift für Anglistick und Amerikanistik: a quarterly of language, literature and culture*, vol. 47 (1999), 218–22). On the gender issue in Barker's trilogy, see also Harris ('Compulsory masculinity, Britain and the Great War: the literary-historical work of Pat Barker', *Critique*, vol. 39 (1998)).

22. Thus in *Brother to Dragons*, Charles and Eric are haunted by childhood memories, and ample references to archaeology introduce the issue of cultural remembering in general. In Barker's trilogy, especially in *The Ghost Road*, Rivers's own repression of childhood memories and his remembrances of anthropological study in Melanesia take the theme of remembering beyond the problems of his traumatised patients.

23. The same link between digging for English prehistory and the modern trench war is drawn in Adam Thorpe's *Ulverton* (London: Minerva, 1992), chapter 10, 'Treasure'.

24. The idea is not new, however, and perhaps inspired by Timothy Findley's *The Wars* (1977). The problem of accessing 1914–18 across a generation gap is also addressed in Julian Barnes's short story 'Tunnel' from *Cross Channel* (London: Cape, 1996). In the year 2015, as the European Parliament plans to 'rationalise the First World War cemeteries' (p. 209), the only way to remember the war will be through the imagination of creative writers like the story's protagonist: 'He, after all, was meant to thrive on knowing and not knowing, on the fruitful misprision, the partial discovery and the resonant fragment' (p. 206).

10

'Charm, Bowler, Umbrella, Leather Boots': Remaking *The Avengers*

Stephen Longstaffe

To judge from the responses to the 1998 film *The Avengers*, one thing you should not do is mess with the postmodern past. Critics and *Avengers* fans alike had nothing good to say about the film: 'no story, no dialogue, no content, no point, no good', 'this film is an insult to cinema', 'a big fat gob of maximum crapulosity'.[1] This is despite considerable alterations made to the film after unfavourable preview screenings in the US. The general release version lacks crucial linking and contextualising material, as is clear both from the original movie screenplay and the website, which carries photos of scenes shot but missing from the final cut. The film was a financial failure, and has since become a byword for 'the archetypal Hollywood disaster'.[2]

One reason for critical sniffiness about the film is that it was seen to signify a characteristically Hollywood combination of voracity and lack of imagination. As a remake of a successful TV series, it sits alongside remakes of European films, costume dramas and formulaic star vehicles as proof of the creative sclerosis of the mainstream. Philip French, for example, identified *The Avengers* as part of history repeating itself as 'big screen spin-off': 'in the wake of major movies inspired by *Star Trek*, *The Brady Bunch*, *Mission: Impossible*, *The Saint* and *Lost In Space*, the whirligig of time brings in *The Avengers*'.[3] If these films are 'spin-offs', however, they are clearly different in kind from the *X-Files* movie (1998) (or, for that matter, the TV spin-off of 1995's *Clueless*). In the latter cases, the 'original' audience still exists and the 'spin-off' product is simply an attempt to repeat the success of the source film in a different medium. The films listed by French seek rather to reconceive and recombine the elements of their originals (actual or implied) for a new audience.

Some remakes seek to update their originals in a fairly straight-forward way, ensuring that they fit a contemporary audience's expectations in terms of hardware or special effects. Others, recognising that one generation's sublime is the next generation's ridiculous, have a more critical attitude to their subject matter. *The Brady Bunch Movie* (1995), for example, re-imagines the original's down-home American family of the 1970s as a kind of latter-day Addams Family, standing in the same relation to its original as Uncle Fester, Lurch and the others did to the terrors of the 1930s generation. For both, the animating question is 'How did people take this seriously?' These remakes are both satirical commentaries on changing fictional conventions, and forms of generational one-upmanship.

The *Avengers* movie, however, fits neither of these paradigms. While most of the TV series mentioned above by French were committed to realism, within the limits of their respective generic conventions, the 1960s *Avengers* in its 'classic' incarnation was heavily committed to camp, pastiche and parody. Remaking *The Avengers* therefore involves pastiching the parodic impulse of its 'original'. In this the 1998 film differs from the reappropriations of another iconic camp 1960s series, *Batman*. Tim Burton's two *Batman* films (*Batman* (1989) and *Batman Returns* (1992)) turned the tables on the 1960s, taking Gothic rather than camp as their key to the original comic's excesses. Whereas the 1960s TV series implied that the original *Batman* had been taken too seriously, the 1980s films countered that the original *Batman* had not taken itself seriously enough.

Of course, identifying the TV *Avengers* simply as parody misses much of its appeal. For a start, there is its M Appeal, especially as personified in Honor Blackman's Mrs Cathy Gale and Diana Rigg's Mrs Emma Peel. At a time when women in adventure series did little but scream and be rescued, both Gale and Peel employed martial arts against their attackers. More broadly, the sexual and non-sexual dynamics of the Steed–Gale/Peel/King relationships have been widely appreciated for their subtlety and playful pushing of boundaries. Such elements obviously depend to some extent on the performers, and a remake without the original cast finds it hard to reproduce some of the original's key virtues. Some of the animus directed at the 1998 film was clearly rooted in the perception that, for example, Uma Thurman is nothing like a Dame Diana Rigg.

Along with a different cast came a retreat from the 1960s *Avengers*'s playfulness regarding gender. Screenplay writer Don Macpherson's reading of the original TV series is that 'over and above everything else, *The Avengers* was really a romance about an unconsummated love affair'.[4] The TV show certainly hinted about the on- and off-screen relationships between Steed and Mrs Gale or Mrs Peel, but was more playfully indeterminate in its commitment to love (and, indeed, non-consummation) as a central dynamic. When Patrick Macnee was selling the show to US TV executives in the 1960s, *his* summary was that '*The Avengers* is about a man in a bowler hat and a woman who flings men over her shoulders'.[5] The 1998 *Avengers*, by contrast, opted for more traditional gender roles, splitting Mrs Peel into a Good Emma (who was not violent) and a cloned Bad Emma (who was). Good Emma practised her fencing against Steed, but only used martial arts once, on parallel wires suspended several hundred feet above the ground, where it mutated into a kind of aggressive gymnastics. Bad Emma shot Steed several times as well as knocking him out, and used her martial arts skills – presumably derived from her 'original', Good Emma – to kill scientists.[6]

However ambivalent it was about a heroine flinging men about, the 1998 film did keep the bowler hat. That *The Avengers* is particularly associated with this item can be confirmed by noting that in both France and Germany it was included in the show's title. In France it was known as *Melon Chapeau et bottes de cuir* (Bowler Hat and Leather Boots) and in Germany *Mit Schirm, Charme, und Melone* (With Umbrella, Charm and Bowler). The bowler hat is a particularly appropriate symbol for *The Avengers*, given its status as a signifier of both High Englishness and surrealism, the combination of which is one of the show's (and the film's) most interesting features. Steed's Englishness of dress and manner, combined with the show's budget-driven tendency to set its exterior scenes in those prettier parts of the rural English home counties near to the studios, ensured that, visually, the show was strongly differentiated from other mid-1960s espionage/adventure shows such as *Batman* or *The Man from UNCLE*. Indeed, as Toby Miller perceptively notes, 'in many ways, *The Avengers*' clothes and accessories *were* the gadgets that marked them out from US rivals'.[7] The show's construction of images of England and Englishness during its 'classic' period was clearly influenced by the requirements of the American market, where the show was networked from the fourth series onwards. Toby Miller reports Patrick Macnee commenting that once the show began to be made in the knowledge that it would be sold to the States (that is, from the fifth series, which was the first to be made in colour) he felt he was working for a US network.[8]

However, the show was sold to the US well after the Steed persona was established. Although at first Macnee's Steed visually resembled Ian Hendry's Dr Keel, he quickly mutated into a quasi-Edwardian dandy once he became the show's lead male character. Steed 'embodied tradition and all that people associated with the British way of life'

> gracious living; a London home full of family heirlooms and handsome antiques; a cultivated appreciation of food, wine, horseflesh and pretty women; proficiency at gentlemanly sports such as fencing, archery and polo; exquisite tailoring; a high-handed way with underlings and an endearing eccentricity which manifested itself in such preferences as driving a vintage Bentley convertible and fighting with a swordstick, rolled umbrella or any other handy implement, rather than the more obvious weapons.[9]

Some of this was due to old Etonian Patrick Macnee, but equally important was the show's overall vision of 'Avengersland'. In the words of writer and producer Brian Clemens, this was a 'carefully contrived, *dateless* fantasy world depicting a Britain of bowlers and brollies, of charm and muffins for tea, a Britain long since gone – if it ever really existed'.[10] This fantasy world, Clemens notes,

> admitted to only one class ... and that was the upper. As a fantasy, we would not show a uniformed policeman or a coloured man. And you would not see anything so common as blood in *The Avengers*. Had we introduced a coloured man or a policeman, we would have had the yardstick of social reality and that would have made the whole thing quite ridiculous. Alongside a bus queue of ordinary men-in-the-street, Steed would have become a caricature.[11]

Though the show has often been praised for refusing stereotypical TV female personas for Cathy Gale and Emma Peel, there were few black or working-class characters. Trinidadian actor Edric Connor played a gang leader in the third series episode 'The Gilded Cage' before Clemens took over as co-producer, but the show as a whole is summed up in the words of Paul Cornell: 'right up to when the series ended, its most prominent black man was Honor'.[12] It is difficult to deny Cornell's point that 'the apartheid of *Avengers* England' could have been avoided by simply casting more black actors, and the absence of black people limits the conception of Englishness on offer in the show.

The presence onscreen of black actors is a different issue from the presence of working-class characters. However clichéd the character played, a black actor is not simply pretending to be black. But to represent the working class it is not necessary for the actor to belong to that class. For working-class characters, therefore, the alternative to exclusion was not a representation in which authenticity was a necessary component; something that the show's roots in spy and SF TV genres in any case militated against. The low budget required that every person shown was foreground rather than background: as Brian Clemens said, 'If you were in shot, you were in the plot.'[13] This refused the common division of actors into cast and extras, itself a form of exclusive representation. The emptiness of both interior and exterior scenes, the latter often focusing on Steed's classic car outside his London mews flat or on traffic-free roads, signalled a world where there was no such thing as the masses or the crowd. More generally, it emphasised that Avengersland constructed rather than copied its England and Englishness.[14]

These constructions were not produced in isolation. *The Avengers*'s version of England and Englishness grew from and responded dynamically to other imaginations of nationality in the 1960s. Some of the most important and internationally popular of these were the James Bond movies. Although *The Avengers* began before the Bond films, many of its features can be productively considered as dialog- ically related to them. Sometimes the show copied the films, as when Steed's bowler hat became a weapon like Oddjob's in *Goldfinger* (1964). Both Honor Blackman and Diana Rigg were 'Bond girls' (the latter in *On Her Majesty's Secret Service* (1969), along with the 1970s *New Avengers* actress Joanna Lumley). Blackman actually left the show in order to appear in *Goldfinger*. Her defection was jokingly recycled in the fourth series episode 'Too Many Christmas Trees', in which Steed receives a Christmas card from Mrs Gale and wonders aloud, 'What *can* she be doing in Fort Knox?'

Casting aside, the relationship between *The Avengers* and the Bond films can be seen as critical. Bond is self-consciously opposed to the 'gentleman spy' genre in which *The Avengers* was, albeit knowingly, rooted, while *The Avengers* raises an ironic eyebrow at the 'modern' simplicities of the Bond world. Unlike the sexually irresistible Bond, Steed's confident charm most clearly signified his class background rather than his sexual attractiveness. Bond's professionalism and classlessness indicated a break with the past, and the films' variety of geographical settings implied that he was part of a new, post-Imperial, meritocratic elite with, as Michael Denning suggests, a 'licence to look' at both women and 'peripheral' places.[15] Mrs Peel and Mrs Gale, being anthropologists, both also had a licence to look, in contrast to Steed, whose expertise and horizons were limited by his class positioning. He was far less intellectual or knowledgeable than either of his female colleagues.

Ian Fleming's Bond was eventually revealed not to be English at all (in Fleming's 1964 *You Only Live Twice* he is identified as half-Scot, half-Swiss). Despite this, and spending almost all of his time in other parts of the world, Bond defended a Britain metonymically represented by a completely English establishment. Avengersland, on the contrary, was definitely English rather than British – and London/Home Counties English at that. The show was concerned with the rituals, fabric and institutions of this specific world rather than exploring national 'character'. Just as the restricted social milieu of classic interwar English detective fiction allowed the development of its puzzle element, *The Avengers*'s social and geo-graphical exclusivity functioned as part of its visual and verbal playfulness, which was inimical to realism. Ironically, this playfulness was more up-to-date, in terms of the emergent 1960s aesthetic, than the Bond films' attempt to update genre conventions by making them acceptably realistic. Indeed, Toby Miller identifies *The Avengers* as an early example of postmodern TV, featuring 'a superfluity of screen palimpsests that are excessive for the needs and capacities of a single story'.[16] The show knowingly recycled pulp and other plots, and often parodied films and TV, as episode titles like 'The Girl from Auntie', 'Mission ... Highly Improbable', and 'The Superlative Seven' indicate. Its High English parody should be understood as both a stylistic and a critical response to Bond's relative straightforwardness, which, if it critiqued anything, was focused on the communist Them.

Bond recognised 'our' diversity only in an Establishment form, in the guise of the Q's eccentricity, which was harnessed to the practical context of producing gadgets and weapons for the forthcoming mission. The madmen, whether scientists or otherwise, were foreign. *The Avengers*, though it began as a conventional enough spy series, by the fourth and fifth series more or less repudiated its own Cold War paranoia (and Bond's more glamorous variant) and began to parody it. It situated the threat to the state in a non-realist context, produced an agent (Steed) whose unreconstructed aristocracy was itself legible as a species of eccentricity, and set itself within an England infested with eccentrics planning to take something or somebody over. But the difference between Bond and *The Avengers* is most clearly visible in their respective treatments of gender. The issue is nicely focused by the fact that Bond took two of its female leads from the TV series. But Mrs Gale and Mrs Peel are not simply pursued by Steed (if they are pursued at all), but work with (not *for*) him. Neither are agents. Avengersland, unlike Bondworld, has room for male/female friendship. In this light, the international success of *The Avengers* indicates a cheering global receptiveness to contra-Bond material.

But if the most interesting and entertaining elements of the 1960s TV show were produced through parodic interrogation of 1960s TV genres and Bond movies, where does that leave the 1998 remake?

Interestingly, long after Bond began to parody itself, the 1998 film includes several knowing nods to the old adversary. Grace Jones, a Bond villain, sings the closing credits tune in a style reminiscent of Shirley Bassey. The film's plot involves the taking over of the world via control not of oil, space or the Internet, but the weather, though the fourth series of *The Avengers* got there first: the episode 'A Surfeit of H_2O' features a cloud-seeding villain called 'Sturm'. And, most obviously, the role of the megalomaniac Bond-villain is taken by Sean Connery himself, who revels in his Scottishness (he is dressed in kilt and sporran to deliver his ultimatum to the world, flanked by bagpipers) and boasts a name (Sir August de Winter) to rival the silliest of the Bond-girls'.

But the 1998 *Avengers* is dialogically engaged not only with TV genre conventions and the 1990s version of Bond, but, crucially, with other contemporary representations of English identity. One of the main principles behind the cuts to the preview version seems to have been the removal of the kind of sex and violence that tilted the movie toward the action genre. Bad Emma killing, Sir August slicing up scientists, the cloned Bad Emma being explicitly jealous of Good Emma, and rather a lot of explosions – all these appear in Macpherson's original screenplay. The cuts in turn refocused the film on the heritage of Englishness. Indeed, the 1960s series' playful Englishness is revisited and intensified. The film packs in as many Hollywood signifiers of Englishness as possible – country houses, mazes and gentlemen's clubs; Jags and Minis; red telephone boxes and London buses; croquet and tea; City suits and bowler hats. This relatively simple use of 'English' signifiers is, however, supplemented by a second layer of mocking or affectionate throwaway references – to Lewis Carroll, Edward Lear, Narnia, the TV dramatisation of *Brideshead Revisited* (1982) and Hammer movies. Beneath the internationally recognised signifiers of Englishness, the England of Swinging London and country houses, there is another layer. Mother (a man, as in the TV series) tells Father (a woman), 'Nothing's impossible, Father. I often think of six impossible things before breakfast' – a quotation from Carroll's *Through The Looking Glass* (1871). Drifting along the Thames in a bubble after vanquishing Sir August, Steed begins a quotation from Edward Lear's 'The Owl and the Pussycat' (1871), which Mrs Peel continues: 'The owl and the pussycat went to sea—' '—In a beautiful pea-green boat'. Before Bad Emma's first assault on Steed, she appears out of a snowstorm like the Queen in C.S. Lewis's *The Lion, The Witch and The Wardrobe* (1950). On the one hand, these references to classic English children's texts are part of the same retro-Englishness as the film's classic cars, stately homes and cod-Victoriana. On the other hand, they acknowledge the centrality of children's fantasy fiction to formative understandings of English national identity. For the many readers of such fiction, their first imagined English communities have fewer humans than non-humans – motoring toads, bears of very little brain, big friendly giants.

This is not to imply that such 'inside' references place Englishness as infantile. Rather, they recognise the diachronic aspects to the imagination of national community, as a process of construction and interpellation beginning in childhood. This understanding of the continuing reproduction of changing senses of Englishness provides an instructive contrast with another, far more popular, film ostensibly engaging with similar territory, *Austin Powers: The Spy Who Shagged Me* (1999). In part it is a Swinging London/James Bond parody which uses some of the same iconic props as *The Avengers*. But here they are just props. No English locations are used. A mockup of swinging London is constructed from stock footage and picture-postcard images – Union Jacks, red telephone boxes, London buses, zebra crossings, guardsmen in bearskins, policemen. That it is a construction is unpacked at length. The Swinging London street is shown to be a set built in the middle of nowhere. As Powers speeds past a red telephone box in the same (clearly non-English) nowhere, he remarks to his companion, 'You know, what's remarkable is how much England looks in no way like Southern California.' These

'England on the cheap' jokes rapidly wear thin, because such coach-tour icons are primarily signifiers of English difference to the outside world rather than being strongly cathected by locals. This is not to claim that *The Avengers* constructs a 'deep Englishness' in contrast to *Austin Powers*'s 'surface Englishness'. Both are concerned with stock English surfaces; the difference is in the variety and ownership of the surfaces on display. The synchronic, snapshot-Englishness in *Austin Powers* is entirely accessible to anybody who has visited London as a conventional tourist; the Englishness of *The Avengers* is constructed for a different audience with a different relationship to English culture.

Taking its cue from the series, *The Avengers* film makes comic use of postmodern techniques. It playfully gestures towards the world outside the film, by casting Ralph Fiennes as a parody of the English gent he so successfully portrays elsewhere, and asking Uma Thurman to test her English accent to destruction with the line 'How now brown cow' (if the film had not been so savagely cut we would also have heard her say the shortest sentence incorporating all the letters of the English alphabet, 'The quick brown fox jumped over the lazy dog'). As in the TV series, there are other kinds of in-joke, referring to both films and the real world. Connery dies as his character does in *Highlander* (1986); Mrs Peel fights a villain swinging from high-tension cables, as in the Bond film *Moonraker* (1979); images and lines are quoted from *Blade Runner* (1982). Teddy bears appear, not, as in *Brideshead Revisited*, trailed behind wistful Oxford undergraduates, but as full-suit disguises for the scientist-conspirators of the Prospero/BROLLY alliance. Visually, the film presents the same mix of country houses and London scenes as the series, with the added twist that many of them are well-known public places rather than anonymous locations in the Home Counties. *The Avengers* was filmed at the Royal Naval College at Greenwich, Windsor Great Park, Syon House, Hatfield House, Blenheim Palace, the Lloyd's building and Stowe School, while other scenes used mock-ups of Trafalgar Square and Big Ben. The makers even used Richard Rogers's own flat for Mrs Peel's home. The use of larger and grander locations intensifies the TV series' characteristic 'emptiness', and emphasises the antirealist aesthetic of the project. It also opposes the film to contemporary appropriations of these locations for the heritage industry, one of the enabling factors for which is costume drama's representations of England and Englishness. Costume drama, in its explanation of how life was lived in these kinds of places, focuses on domestic interiority rather than their power to awe. *The Avengers*, in putting a mad scientist with a plan for world domination into a stately home, recognises the megalomania behind creating and living in such buildings.

The show's antirealist aesthetic emerges in other details that show its preference for the quoted over the quotidian. People in teddy bear suits populate the Lloyd's building (a nice take on that building's iconic modernity). Sir August's first appearance is preceded by a shot of a room filled with 1500 recently shaken snow shakers. His orchids have giant lenses in front of them through which we see from the orchid's point of view the humans admiring it. Mrs Peel encounters an Escher staircase trying to escape from Sir August's stately home, the aptly named Hallucinogen Hall. These variously impressive or playful settings are juxtaposed with the shabbiness of the Ministry for which Steed works – a range of gloomy underground corridors heated by a wood-burning stove. Mother, the ostensible head of the outfit, is a scruffy chain-smoker covered in dandruff, fag ash and macaroon crumbs. Steed the employee, on the other hand, is dressed by Savile Row. This productive disjunction with Mother is part of the film's modification of Macnee's original Steed, who, though equally stylish, was undeniably from the English aristocracy. Though Fiennes's Steed is rich and patronises gentlemen's outfitters, the film does its best to present his class simply as a source of style. His interests outside the immediate adventure are seemingly limited, like Mrs Peel's, to chess, who, though equally stylish (and, to judge from her apartment, equally rich), is similarly classy without being aristocratic. The poster for the movie, which featured Steed as city gent and Peel in a leather catsuit, carried the slogan 'saving the world in style'.

There are also jokes that are simply jokes. Or rather, the film employs, as the series did, the kind of understated wit organically related to a comic view of English formality (that is, as something other than an indication of a desperately repressed and impoverished inner life). After stumbling into a building inhabited by scientists in large teddy bear suits, Mrs Peel is attacked by her double, Bad Emma, who is also wearing a bear suit. Steed arrives in time to register the two faces side by side, after which Bad Emma escapes and the following exchange occurs:

PEEL: Just in time to save me from myself.
STEED: Are you all right? I thought I was seeing double.
PEEL: That makes two of us.

The 1960s TV series began from many of the same elements as Bond films, but used them to construct an alternative perspective, rooted in a past that Bond repudiated, on national and gender identities and the pleasures of genre. The film continues this strategy. Producer Jerry Weintraub states of the film's 'Avengersland', 'We're in London and it's the sixties, but it's the sixties as though they hadn't gone away, they've just been going on for a very long time'.[17] In other words, 'Avengersland' is an idyllic alternate world in which the England and Englishness of over 30 years' worth of Merchant–Ivory films, Jane Austen adaptations, and TV versions of 'classic' nineteenth- and twentieth-century English novels simply *have never existed*. As with Bond, the 1998 film takes the materials used by other constructions of England and Englishness – race, gender, money, class, style – but constructs them so that, like the Lloyd's building, their constructedness is always visible.

This is not to deny that the film is nostalgic. But its nostalgia is not for the vanished world of its icons of Englishness, but for the TV series on which it is based. Macpherson's script is full of references to old *Avengers* episodes. It quotes, for example, the Peel–Steed fencing duel of the first Mrs Peel episode, 'The Town of No Return'; Steed's helping Mrs Gale with her tight leather boots in 'Death of a Batman'; and the line introducing all the fifth series shows, 'Mrs Peel, we're needed'. Patrick Macnee, the original Steed, even has a walk-on (or rather a shimmer-on) part as an invisible man ('Learnt the trick in camouflage. Till the accident made rather a mess of things'). But the film's pastiche of these and other 'original' elements can be seen as simple homage (or, as many critics claimed, failed homage) only as long as the postmodern nature of the 1960s TV series – and thus the film itself – is forgotten. Remaking was always part of *The Avengers*.

While it is difficult to avoid comparing the film with that of the best of the TV series, it is important to remember that, in terms of presenting England and Englishness, the two have different projects. The Irish poet Patrick Kavanagh developed in the 1940s and 1950s an aesthetic of the parochial, which he contrasted with the 'provincial' which has 'no mind of his own; he does not trust what his eyes see until he has heard what the metropolis – towards which his eyes are turned – has to say on any subject'. Provincialism, as Kavanagh defines it, bedevils many imaginings of Englishness (especially those produced elsewhere), with the United States functioning as the metropolis toward which the provincial imagination is oriented. Both incarnations of *The Avengers* might be said to be parochial, in Kavanagh's sense of an opposition, rooted in inside knowledge, to the merely provincial.[18] Both resist the American – or American-centred – construction of England and Englishness as provincial with regard to the centrality of the US (though both have their limitations, particularly in their virtually all-white casts). The film is not designed to make instant sense to audiences uninterested in Englishness. Its ironic casting of Englishmen like comedian Eddie Izzard and the legendarily wasted singer Shaun Ryder as non-speaking heavies is just one example of the ways in which the film addresses itself to insiders. But while the TV series dialogically engaged with Bond's particular brand of realist modernity, the 1998 film's most powerful contemporary companions in imagining Englishness are backward-looking, particularly towards the long Imperial century overflowing both sides of the nineteenth. The heritage films are themselves an attempt to look back before the Americanisation of Britain, a project the *Avengers* shares but critiques. The crucial element of this critique is its refusal of realism. It is important to the *Avengers*'s kind of parochiality – rooted in a variety of references intentionally incomprehensible in Peoria – that it is both knowing and whimsical about representations of Englishness, including its own. In doing so, it allows the imagination back into the imagined community of England.

Thanks to Jim Riley for discussions about both the film and the series, and for access to his collection of cult TV materials.

Notes

1. From the *Sunday Times*, *Daily Mail*, and *New York Post* respectively, as quoted in Nick Paton Walsh, 'Putting the kinky boot in', *Guardian*, 21 August 1998.
2. Adam Smith, 'A film you can afford to miss', *Observer*, 16 April 2000.
3. Philip French, 'Film of the Week: *The Avengers*', *Observer*, 16 August 1998.
4. Don Macpherson, *The Avengers: Original Movie Screenplay* (London: Titan Books, 1998), p. ix.
5. Patrick Macnee and Marie Cameron, *Blind in One Ear: The Avengers returns* (San Francisco: Mercury House, 1989), p. 242.

6. One of the film's 'missing scenes' showed Good Emma getting into the exclusive men's club Boodles by using martial arts on the doorman. Macpherson, *The Avengers*, p. 15; <http://www.sierra-safari.com/avmissing.html>

7. Toby Miller, *The Avengers* (London: British Film Institute, 1997), p. 42.

8. Ibid., p. 19.

9. Dave Rogers, *The Complete Avengers* (London: Boxtree, 1989), p. 88.

10. Brian Clemens, 'Foreword' to ibid., p. 9.

11. Rogers, *Complete*, p. 90.

12. Paul Cornell, Martin Day and Keith Topping, *The Avengers Dossier: the definitive unauthorised guide* (London: Virgin, 1998), p. 349.

13. Miller, *The Avengers*, p. 12.

14. Both the 1998 film's producer Jerry Weintraub and production designer Stuart Craig saw the emptiness of the TV series as suggesting the paintings of Magritte. See Dave Rogers, *The Avengers: the making of the movie* (London: Titan Books, 1998), pp. 14, 34.

15. Michael Denning, *Cover Stories: narrative and ideology in British spy thrillers* (London: Routledge & Kegan Paul, 1987), pp. 91–113.

16. Miller, *The Avengers*, p. 119.

17. Rogers, *The Avengers*, p. 14.

18. Antoinette Quinn, *Patrick Kavanagh: born-again Romantic* (Dublin: Gill and Macmillan, 1993), p. 199. See also her discussion of Kavanagh's parochialism, pp. 195–254.

11

Forbidden Planet and the Retrospective Attribution of Intentions

Judith Buchanan

The popular American science-fiction film *Forbidden Planet* (1956) is widely acknowledged as a creative reworking of the narrative of Shakespeare's *The Tempest*. The parallels between the two texts are not difficult to discern. In summary, these relate to:

- the nature and status of the isolated territory
- the possessive relationship of the central magus figure to his virginal daughter
- the scientist-magus's relationship to the untameable creature who represents his own baser instincts
- the virginal daughter's first engagements with the attractions of a world beyond her father
- the rendering of a mythic tale with an overlaid contemporary political resonance.

My concern here is not to expand on these, but rather to query what they may legitimately be taken to signify about the nature of the relationship between the two texts.[1] In pursuing this question I trace the film's reception from the 1950s to the 1990s. I also introduce a discussion of the horror film *Island of Lost Souls* (1932) as an illuminating point of comparison. Whereas *Forbidden Planet* is widely regarded as a version of *The Tempest*, *Island of Lost Souls*, despite its considerable Shakespearean parallels, has no history of being discussed in these terms. This is, I contend, testimony as much to the erratic vagaries of critical attention as to anything substantive about the Shakespearean or non-Shakespearean character of either film.

Bob Carlton's popular stage musical, derivatively entitled *Return to the Forbidden Planet*, first performed in 1990 and advertised as

'Shakespeare's Forgotten Rock'n'Roll Masterpiece', both trades upon and, in doing so, confirms the Shakespearean association of the 1956 film. The stage production features characters named Dr Prospero, Miranda, Ariel, Bosun and Dr Tempest and includes extensive quotation and misquotation from *The Tempest* as well as from other Shakespeare plays. It leaves no room for ambiguity about the deliberateness of its references to Shakespeare, so consolidating the impression, if only accidentally, that this too is what its inspiration, *Forbidden Planet*, had done. In the case of *Forbidden Planet*, however, there are grounds for questioning this.

Forbidden Planet makes no mention of *The Tempest* in its title or credit sequences and was not advertised with any claim of a Shakespeare association during its early exhibition runs or in its press releases. As a landmark production for MGM, and a costly one, it was much reviewed in the year of its release. *Films in Review, Monthly Film Bulletin, Variety, Motion Picture Herald, Film Daily, Hollywood Reporter*, the *New York Times, Kinematograph Weekly* and *Today's Cinema* were, for example, among those publications that reviewed the film between its preview (22 February 1956) and late June of the same year. Not one of these contemporary reviews mentions a Shakespearean resonance to the film.

Those reviewers who considered what might have inspired the film produced speculative descriptions such as this from the *New York Times*: 'Weird science fiction based primarily on fact, on present experimentation and on fertile imagination'.[2] Those who considered the film's possible literary or dramatic precedents were still not struck by any Shakespearean affinities, tending to arrive at more recent or populist models instead: 'a King Kong of space'; 'Walter Pidgeon play[s] the Jekyll-and-Hyde scholar'.[3] Even when in May 1956 Bosley Crowther, with unconscious irony, drew attention to the appropriateness of the Globe movie theatre as the film's New York venue, he clearly only intended that 'appropriateness' to refer to the planetary associations of the theatre's name for the showing of a space fantasy rather than to anything about Shakespearean playhouses.[4] Even an accident of location that might, with hindsight, have been expected to sensitise an audience to any latent Shakespearean narrative patterning in the film still triggered no spark of recognition among critics or reviewers. The film was received as an innovative and impressive work of cinema in terms of its ambitious special effects, its awe-inspiring sets, its groundbreaking use of robotics and its original soundtrack. Any suggestion of a

Shakespeare association, however, seems to have been entirely absent from contemporary readings.

The earliest published comment connecting *Forbidden Planet* to *The Tempest* that I have been able to trace was made by Kingsley Amis in 1961. In *New Maps of Hell* he suggested that there had been 'a work oddly omitted' from previous considerations of the sources for science fiction in general and *Forbidden Planet* in particular. While the *Tempest*, he claimed, could only be considered 'a very dilute and indirect influence on science fiction', it was nevertheless 'a distant anticipation':

> On a cruder level, the eccentric scientist-recluse and his beautiful daughter are an almost woefully familiar pair of stereotypes in all but the most recent science fiction, and, incidentally, large areas of what I might call the *Tempest* myth reappear in one of the best science fiction films. The title was *Forbidden Planet*...[5]

Amis's discussion of the play as a previous 'omission' in such studies, combined with his own slightly diffident choice of words – drawing attention only 'incidentally' to the correspondences between play and film – would seem to confirm this as the first expression of a new idea being tried upon the reading public.

Despite the popularity of *New Maps of Hell,* Amis's particular claim that *Forbidden Planet* was partially indebted to *The Tempest* was not immediately embraced by the critical establishment.[6] Rather, once given its first, slightly tentative airing, the idea then percolated gradually through the critical community so that later critics were not even aware that it had, or needed to have had, an author and moment of first saying. By 1969 the idea of a Shakespearean connection was gaining in currency:

> *Forbidden Planet* is a superior sci-fier in which some discern parallels to *The Tempest*. The planet called Altaire in this film is likened to the magical island of *The Tempest*, and the character called Morbius, played by Walter Pidgeon, is thought of as a modern Prospero. Ariel is a super-robot: Caliban a tellurous demon somewhat resembling a tree-sloth.[7]

In the following year John Baxter published a survey of science fiction in the cinema, significantly entitling his chapter on 1950s Hollywood science fiction 'Springtime for Caliban'.[8] Throughout the early 1970s *The Tempest* was then regularly discussed alongside *Forbidden Planet* with the unthinking confidence of a well-rehearsed, uncontested argument. The weight of critical writing even implied that the association had *from the first* been an integral part of the film's conception and reception. This critical trend, retrospectively investing the film with intentions it did not communicate at the time, has persisted. And from 1970 onwards the critical line has been as consistently attentive to the Shakespearean association as it had been negligent of it in the film's early years.

In 1976, for example, discussing the film's initial reception, Douglas Brode wrote: 'Critics who entered the theatre expecting another routine outer space adventure were shocked to discover that this film bore an eerie resemblance to Shakespeare's *The Tempest*.'[9] Similarly in 1977, James Parish and Michael Pitts, historians of the film science fiction genre, wrote that in *Forbidden Planet* 'the audience found an intelligent blending of the wild creature storyline and a retelling of Shakespeare's play *The Tempest*'.[10] In 1982 Philip Strick went as far as to draw distinctions between the type of Shakespearean attention that he claimed the film *had* received in 1956 and that which it *should* have received: 'The hit of the film was Robby the Robot, not the star, Walter Pidgeon, and while critics made passing allusions to *The Tempest*, it was overlooked that Shakespeare's play had already dealt with disenchantment.'[11] The evidence, however, suggests that film audiences of the time were not 'shocked ... [by] an eerie resemblance to ... *The Tempest*', did not find in the film 'a retelling of ... *The Tempest*', and overlooked considerably more that was arguably Shakespearean in it than the single theme of disenchantment: Shakespeare was not partially but entirely absent from their frame of reference.

Once established, however, this revisionist critical tendency – remembering for example 'passing allusions to *The Tempest*' where there had been none – has passed so authoritatively into the popular mythology surrounding the film that it seems to have entirely escaped sceptical interrogation or verification. In 1993, for example, in typically populist style, John Douglas Eames and Ronald Bergan turned the film's Shakespeare association into a sensationalist case of unscrupulous artistic conduct:

Without so much as a by your leave to Shakespeare's agent, *Forbidden Planet* pinched the whole plot of *The Tempest* and turned it into a sci-fi epic starring Robby the Robot. And what's more, it credited Irving Block and Allen Adler for the basis of Cyril Hume's script.[12]

This tongue-in-cheek accusation of plagiarism partly depends for its humour upon the assumption that with or without a specific credit, spectators would have been left in no doubt about the *real* (Shakespearean) source for the film. The contemporary evidence to support such an assumption is noticeable only by its absence.

However, it is not the case that the 1956 reviews have never come under scrutiny. John Brosnan, for example, who in 1991 wrote, 'Not many sf films can claim that Shakespeare did the original treatment but *Forbidden Planet* can – it is based on *The Tempest*,' pointed out in the same publication that contemporary reviewers missed the intimations of an incestuous relationship between Morbius and his daughter.[13] Brosnan's consideration of the original reviews, and observation of something absent from them, makes it the more astonishing that the assumption persisted, even in Brosnan himself, that those same reviews were suffused with comment on the film's similarities to the Shakespeare play. Even consideration of the reviews did not produce a recognition of the striking absence of reference to Shakespeare in the film's early reception. Rather, the critical orthodoxy asserting an early association has instead been reinforced through regular repetition.[14]

Since 1970, therefore, the 'actual' spectators, to use Susan Suleiman's and Inge Crosman's terms, of *Forbidden Planet* (who in 1956 paid money to watch the film and did not, it would seem, identify anything Shakespearean in the experience) have been conveniently reconfigured as 'ideal' spectators (who would have recognised every possible latent allusion in the text and who were therefore at once struck, as Douglas Brode has claimed, by the film's 'eerie resemblance' to *The Tempest*).[15] Such an ideal spectatorship is, however, an interpretative construct of a later period, revealing much about modern tendencies to project contemporary patterns of critical reception back onto earlier contexts. However, it is actively misleading about the film's actual reception at the time of its release.

The possibility that the Shakespeare parallels in *Forbidden Planet* were deliberately evoked cannot, of course, be wholly discounted. Indeed in 1975, Irving Block, who had co-written the story upon which the screenplay was based, emerged from the shadows to tell *Cinéfantastique* that it had been he who had 'suggested they use Shakespeare's *The Tempest* as a premise on which to build the science fiction story'.[16] Until this point nobody associated with the film seems to have publicised such a connection, or even to have mentioned it casually to a reporter. Since those members of the production team who might have been able to discuss the film's narrative origins (director Fred McLeod Wilcox, producer Nicholas Nayfack, co-writer Allen Adler, screenplay writer Cyril Hume) were already dead, Block's late claim, made 19 years after the film's first release, cannot be contested. On the other hand, it lacks documentary or anecdotal corroboration from the time of the film's production. And even if true in relation to the original story, this in itself would not necessarily make it also true for the film. It seems more probable that the lack of comment on the subject from the studio and production team either at the time of the film's release or in the years that followed indicates a genuine innocence on their part (if not also on Block's) of the narrative similarities between their film and an earlier work, however prestigious that work might be. Nevertheless, correspondences between the film and the play are easy to discern. If the later work need not necessarily be considered a *deliberate* emulation of the former, an alternative means of accounting for the many parallels needs to be found.

One possible explanation for this is provided by the Jungian theory about archetypal narrative forms. Jung claimed that a small body of archetypal narratives which embody and so satisfy fundamental human narrative cravings resurface repeatedly across social and temporal boundaries. These fundamental narratives are constantly in circulation in one form or another. By a process of unknowing transmission, they can be absorbed into a cultural awareness of the forms that stories may most pleasingly take, and so be unconsciously reworked and innocently presented as if new. An individual tale may thereby endure through constant recycling even when a particular telling of it demonstrates no conscious awareness of its affinity with and contribution to a wider tradition. Such a theory of unknowing transmission may account for the close correspondences between *Forbidden Planet* and *The Tempest*. The film uncannily reproduces many elements of Shakespeare's play and explores several of its themes and relationships with remarkable accuracy, but without *necessarily* a conscious awareness of the illustrious dramatic tradition within which it was working.

In a retrospective inquiry of this sort, the vexed question of intentionality cannot long be avoided. A refreshingly eccentric approach

to this question in relation to seemingly imitative texts is offered by
Stanley Cavell in his critical analysis of Fellini's film *La Strada* (1954).
Ronald Dworkin has summarised Cavell's argument thus:

> Stanley Cavell ... [has shown] how even the concrete, detailed
> intentions of an artist can be problematic. He notices that a
> character in Fellini's film *La Strada* can be seen as a reference to the
> Philomel legend, and he asks what we need to know about Fellini
> in order to say that the reference was intentional (or, what is
> different, not unintentional). He imagines a conversation with
> Fellini in which the filmmaker says that although he has never
> heard of the story before, it captures the feeling he had about his
> character while filming, that is, that he *now* accepts it as part of the
> film he made. Cavell says that he is inclined in these circum-
> stances to treat the reference as intended. Cavell's analysis ...
> suggests a conception of intention quite different from the crude
> conscious-mental-state conception. An insight belongs to an
> artist's intention, on this view, when it fits and illuminates his
> artistic purposes in a way he would recognise and endorse even
> though he has not already done so...
>
> Cavell's imagined conversation with Fellini begins in Cavell's
> finding the film better if it is read as including a reference to
> Philomel and in his supposing that Fellini could be brought to
> share that view, to *want* the film read that way, to see his
> ambitions better realized by embracing that intention.[17]

Cavell shifts the resonances of the term 'intention' so far away from
its commonly accepted meaning as to make it all but indistinguish-
able from 'interpretation'. That is to say that he seems to remove it
from the province of the author to that of the reader. Despite this
semantic fluidity, however, the central point of the account is clear:
that an interpretative reading of a work of art should not be limited
by consciously acknowledged authorial intentions since that work
may legitimately live beyond these in ways not anticipated at its
moment of composition yet still entirely consistent with the original
artistic vision.

Since, as discussed, no acknowledged intentions about seeking to
make a Shakespearean reference in *Forbidden Planet* have come to
light prior to 1975 (by which time their validity is open to question),
this interpretative model may provide a helpful way of understanding the coincidence of dramatic structure between *The Tempest* and
Forbidden Planet. This may be considered 'intended' within the

framework of intentionality constructed by Cavell since a Shakespeare-infused reading of *Forbidden Planet* has, since 1970, been almost universally seen as 'better realiz[ing]' its artistic purposes.

The case of the 1932 horror film *Island of Lost Souls*, adapted from H.G. Wells's short novel *The Island of Dr Moreau* (1896), provides a useful point of comparison. Wells's novel finds representation for several of *The Tempest*'s narrative elements. In the film adaptation, the narrative was drawn yet closer to the central concerns of the play. Despite the correspondences, the film has never to my knowledge been discussed in conjunction with *The Tempest*. It too, therefore, may be considered as drawing upon *The Tempest* only by a Cavellian interpretative scheme in which the film is retrospectively invested with intentions it did not communicate at the time.

The Island of Dr Moreau relates the story of a highly educated scientist, Dr Moreau, whose secret studies in London proved ethically unacceptable to the establishment. He is therefore banished to an unknown island where he lives out the fantasies and implications of his forbidden scientific experiments into the possibilities of transforming brute animals into civilised human beings. There he is the acknowledged master, having complete control over the other, more primitive, inhabitants of the island by means of a reign of terror. Having survived a shipwreck, Edward Prendick finds himself on this island. Prendick is able to observe how Moreau is deified by the island inhabitants, as, among other things, the controller of 'the lightning-flash' and 'the deep salt sea'.[18] It transpires eventually that the brutish island inhabitants are in fact literally Moreau's creatures in that he has created them by the uncompromising surgical restructuring of animal tissue into human form. He has also then patiently tutored the creatures resulting from this reconstructive surgery in language skills and in 'civilised' codes of behaviour. Moreau describes to Prendick the educative process through which he had put one of his creatures: 'I taught him the rudiments of English, gave him ideas of counting, even made the thing read the alphabet ... He began with a clean sheet, mentally.'[19] From his descriptions of his creations and own creative processes it becomes obvious that Moreau has high hopes of what is possible by way of the suppression of instinct and the elevation of reason: 'This time I will burn out all the animal, this time I will make a rational creature of my own.'[20] Moreau's creatures cannot, however, be permanently diverted from their instinctive drives which, despite all his efforts at tutoring and subjection, finally resurface with devastating results.

The correspondences between the essential situation of Wells's tale and that of *The Tempest* are self-evident. Prospero too is banished from his home to a strange, remote island where he proclaims himself the absolute authority. The reasons for his banishment are similar, in that he too had closeted himself away in the pursuit of hermetic knowledge. Once on the island, Prospero establishes himself as a figure of god-like authority, raises a sea tempest and teaches language to a brutish savage, Caliban, in an attempt to tutor him into an understanding of virtue and civilised values. He too, like Moreau, seems to have worked on the assumption that the savage before him was a *tabula rasa* and so could be inscribed with any moral character he chose. Caliban, however, according to Miranda, proves to be ineducable, inaccessible to 'any print of goodness' (I.ii.354). Prospero, like Moreau, is forced to recognise the failure of his own experiment in the construction of a civilised being when Caliban's insufficiently suppressed instincts, first for sex and later for bloody revenge, surface. Prospero then holds Caliban in an enforced slavery, treating him with contempt and imposing harsh punishments on him for any show of disobedience or resentment. Like Moreau, therefore, Prospero is ultimately disappointed in his own powers to divert nature from its instinctive drives. In the Wells novel, however, the single anarchic Caliban figure has proliferated into a *range* of primitive and ultimately untutorable savages. Moreau's role as creator of these human savages is a translation onto a physical plane of the Shakespearean idea of Caliban as the product of Prospero's dealings with, and language used to, him. Caliban, for example, having been taught language by Prospero, enjoys bitterly spitting it back at him in imitative curses. Whereas Prospero is partly responsible for having made Caliban what he is, Moreau's creatures are literally the product of his handiwork. Thus the essential identity of the Caliban presence, whether in singular or plural form, is recognisable across works as alike in tendencies, influences and dramatic function.

Island of Lost Souls (starring Charles Laughton as Moreau) moves the Wells narrative yet closer to the dramatic interests of *The Tempest*. Most significant of the film's several adjustments of the narrative in the direction of the Shakespeare play is that whereas on the novel's island 'the females were less numerous than the males', in the film there is only one woman, Lota, the most perfect of Moreau's creations.[21] The presence on a remote island of a lone woman who has never seen a civilised man except her elderly male 'creator' generates a highly *Tempest*-like resonance to this island community. Because of her sexual vulnerability Lota needs, and receives, the special protection of Moreau himself, whose care for her is both as tender and as calculating as Prospero's is for Miranda. Moreau decides to expose her to the shipwrecked visitor (Edward Parker in the film), with the deliberate intention of observing her naïve responses to the first young man she has ever seen. His degree of clinical forethought in engineering this meeting is reminiscent of Prospero's approach to the strategically choreographed encounter between Miranda and Ferdinand. Prospero says to Miranda:

> The fringed curtains of thine eye advance,
> And say what thou seest yond ...
> ... This gallant which thou seest
> Was in the wrack; and but he's something stain'd
> With grief (that's beauty's canker) thou mightst call him
> A goodly person...
>
> (I.ii.411–12, 416–19)

Moreau prepares Lota for the social task ahead even more explicitly:

> Lota, I've taught you many things. All that you know I have taught you. I'm going to let you learn something for yourself. A man has come from the sea. I will take you to him. I'm going to leave you alone with him. You may talk with him about anything you please. About the world he comes from ...

What is more, Moreau does not try to veil his purposes even when Parker is present. Having introduced Parker to Lota, he adds, without subtlety, 'She is the only woman on the entire island. Well, I'll leave you two young people together: I've got work to do,' before disappearing from sight in order to watch them, Prospero-fashion, himself unobserved. There is even a suggestion near the end of the film, when a small rescue party, including Parker's fiancée Ruth, appears on the island, that Moreau intends a corresponding experiment in social engineering for an inverse gender pairing, and will force Ruth to mate with one of the beast-men. In each case Moreau plans to exploit the socially and sexually controlled environment which he has created in order to observe how well courtship and mating instincts function when deprived of any instruction or patterns for emulation.

There is a precedent for this duplication of the innocents whose first encounter with a character of the opposite sex may be turned into a source of dramatic interest. In the 1670 Dryden–Davenant collaborative adaptation of *The Tempest*, entitled *The Tempest, or The Enchanted Island*, alongside a Miranda (and in fact a Dorinda) who had never seen a man, another character, Hippolito, was introduced: 'the Counterpart to Shakespear's [sic] Plot, namely that of a Man who had never seen a Woman; that by this means those two Characters of Innocence and Love might the more illustrate and commend each other'.[22] The Miranda-like socially naïve and sexually inexperienced character has, therefore, on more than one occasion been considered a sufficiently effective dramatic device 'to be wondered at' in multiplied form.

The novel's broad correspondences with the Shakespeare play are thus moved closer to it, and to its tradition of adaptation, in the film – and yet still with no deliberate *intention* to mimic or even evoke the substance of *The Tempest*. The distillation of the novel's *several* female innocents created by Moreau down to the film's *single* Miranda-like presence of Lota indicates a pull towards a simplifying of the material in the interests of dramatic and emotional clarity. And from the paring away of some of the novel's more elaborate margins, the more focused narrative of the film emerges looking more Shakespearean in its dramatic interests. *Island of Lost Souls* finds representation for the play's shipwreck, uncharted island and entirely unsocialised virgin, as well as for the imperious/paternal exiled magus figure (Prospero/Dr Moreau) who practises forbidden arts (conjurations/life-transforming surgery), and the primitive savage(s) (Caliban/the beast-men) driven more by instinct than reason who despite all efforts at tutoring cannot easily be accommodated within the 'civilised' sphere of the magus figure. The film's correspondences to the Shakespeare play are therefore considerable. They have not, however, prompted comment. Such stories are apparently able, in some cases, to be in circulation without the need for precise labels of derivation to be attached to them.

I have cited the case of *Island of Lost Souls* to demonstrate that *Forbidden Planet*'s relationship to *The Tempest*, though strong, need not necessarily be *strategic* on the part of its producers. Stories as fundamental and familiar as the one we know most commonly as *The Tempest* find representation constantly in various transmuted forms. Whether they are identified as such or not seems to depend not only upon the strength of the association, but sometimes, less predictably, upon the random accidents of critical attention.

Though the specific process of transmission of the inherited narrative tradition may not be evident in the case of *Forbidden Planet*, it seems plain to contemporary viewers that consciously or unconsciously the film did draw on the same story pool as *The Tempest*. What now seems plain, however, has not always been so. In the 1950s, the particular visual and cultural idioms into which the film translated the inherited narrative were sufficiently new for its Shakespearean correspondences to have been overlooked in favour of a critical absorption in its various innovative special effects. MGM's own trade advertisement for the film certainly made available a wealth of enticing, entirely non-Shakespearean material for critical comment:

> See an electronic blaster vaporize an attacking tiger in mid-air! See an invisible demon hurl an Earthman to fiery destruction! See an uninhibited beauty as she meets young Earthmen for the first time! See the fabulous flying saucer spaceship of 2200 AD – faster than the speed of light! See how the invisible demon smashes buildings and burns itself through steel! See Robby, the Robot, the most amazing technical genius ever devised! See two moons floating in a green sky! See the planet Altair explode into a fiery inferno! See the fabulous inventions of planet people of 2,000,000 years ago! See the thrilling romance of an Earthman and a captive planet goddess! See how the final destruction of the invisible demon is accomplished! Never before on any screen ... Unique! Different![23]

It was the film's proclaimed 'unique[ness]!' and 'differen[ce]!' rather than any familiarity or derivativeness that merited comment in the early days of its release. There was plenty of interesting material to discuss, from the film's pioneering use of visual and aural technologies to its sexualised view of an unsocialised virgin, without critics needing to cite Shakespearean parallels to fill copy. The tone and detail of the reviews from 1956 confirm this. It was only after the slightly dazzled initial interest in the film's special effects had waned that serious consideration of possible narrative parallels found the critical space, or indeed the need, to surface.

This may partially explain how *Forbidden Planet* escaped acknowledgement as a narrative parallel to *The Tempest* during the early years of its exhibition. In many ways, though, this is still an enigma. Anecdotal evidence from people who saw the film in the late 1950s and early 1960s indicates that the claim of a Shakespearean allusion in the film, once made, certainly did not jar with existing readings. It might even have confirmed, as the best ideas do, a common, although previously unformulated, impression of familiarity in the film's narrative. Nevertheless, the obviousness of the correspondence between the film and the play from *our* historical perspective renders it difficult to understand how it could have been unrecognised or ignored from an earlier one. It is perhaps this difficulty in believing that what is now widely recognised might not always have been so that has led many critics retrospectively, and misleadingly, to conjure fictional readings of the 1950s that identified a Shakespearean patterning in the film. The film's early reception, however, was determined by real rather than by subsequently constructed ideal spectators, and those real spectators were struck by nothing in the film sufficiently Shakespearean to merit published comment.

No film in the evolving history of *Tempest* adaptations, perhaps even of Shakespeare adaptations generally, has generated such widespread critical misapprehensions as *Forbidden Planet*. There is an enormous number of films, and narratives in other media, that appear somewhere along a continuum of graduated removes from so ubiquitous a narrative as *The Tempest*. The cut-off point beyond which audiences either fail to identify the resemblance or fail to think it an interpretatively useful referent varies between individual spectators and between spectating communities. *Island of Lost Souls*, however, appears as least as close to *The Tempest* on this continuum as does *Forbidden Planet*; and perhaps even closer. Had it been picked up by an Amis figure, as *Forbidden Planet* was, at a timely moment, it might have received a similar degree of attention as a translated *Tempest* movie. Since it already had an obvious and respectable literary derivation in Wells's novel, however, no one felt the same need to seek out a source narrative beyond that. As the random accidents of critical attention would have it, therefore, *Island of Lost Souls* has escaped the centripetal process by which some popular texts receive a form of establishment validation by being read in the light of classical precedents.

The reconstruction – post-production – of popular texts as versions of classics testifies both to a need to criticise by cited comparison, and to a more specific desire to honour a modern work by drawing it into relationship with an older one already established as canonical. It may be that through the 1960s and 1970s *Forbidden Planet* was recognised as suitable material to feed an establishment urge to draw in popular texts from the wastelands of popular culture towards a canonical centre as a means of investing them with cultural validity. But things change, and even in the academy popular culture has now broadly shed its wasteland associations. Many popular texts have become a legitimate area of serious enquiry in their own right, independent of any claim to a connection with a text of established 'high' culture. In this new, more culturally democratic, climate it remains to be seen whether attributing an intention to mimic a classic to a popular text will continue to be thought value enhancing.

Notes

1. For a fuller discussion of the Shakespearean correspondences in the film, see my discussion of the film forthcoming in *Shakespeare on Film* (London: Longman, 2002). All references to Shakespeare's *Tempest* are taken from Frank Kermode edn, (1954. Reprint London: Methuen, 1979).
2. F.R., *New York Times*, 6 March 1956.
3. *Monthly Film Bulletin*, no. 23 (June 1956), p. 71, and an unreferenced review clip on file in the Library of Congress reading room.
4. Bosley Crowther, *New York Times*, 4 May 1956.
5. Kingsley Amis, *New Maps of Hell* (London: Gollancz, 1961), pp. 29–30. As Amis explains in the introduction to *The Golden Age of Science Fiction* (London: Hutchinson, 1981), *New Maps of Hell* was originally delivered as a series of lectures at Princeton University in 1959.
6. *New Maps of Hell* was enthusiastically reviewed, and sold in sufficient quantities to merit being translated into French, Italian and Spanish within a few years of its first publication.
7. John B. Sewell, 'Shakespeare on Screen II: an updating of our Lillich article of twelve years ago', *Film Review*, 20 (August–September 1969), p. 421.
8. John Baxter, *Science Fiction in the Cinema* (London: Zwemmer, 1970), pp. 102–15.
9. Douglas Brode, *Films of the Fifties* (New York: Carol Publishing Group, 1976), p. 183.
10. James Robert Parish and Michael R. Pitts, *The Great Science Fiction Picture* (Metuchen: Scarecrow, 1977), p. 137.
11. Philip Strick, 'Space invaders', in *Movies of the Fifties*, ed. Ann Lloyd (London: Orbis, 1982), p. 34.

12. John Douglas Eames and Ronald Bergan, *The MGM Story* (London: Hamlyn, 1993), p. 276.
13. John Brosnan, *The Primal Screen: a history of science fiction film* (New York: Little, Brown and Co., 1991), pp. 54–5, 57.
14. See, for example, Sara Martin's essay, 'Classic Shakespeare for all: *Forbidden Planet* and *Prospero's Books*, two screen adaptations of *The Tempest*', in Deborah Cartmell, I.Q. Hunter, Heidi Kaye and Imelda Whelehan (eds), *Classics in Film and Fiction* (London: Pluto, 2000), pp. 34–53.
15. Susan Suleiman and Inge Crosman (eds), *The Reader in the Text* (Princeton: Princeton University Press, 1980), introductory chapter.
16. Steve Rubin, 'Retrospect: *Forbidden Planet*', *Cinéfantastique*, vol 4. no. 1. (Spring 1975), p. 7.
17. Ronald Dworkin, *Law's Empire* (London: Fontana, 1986), pp. 56–7, citing Stanley Cavell, *Must We Mean What We Say?* (New York: Scribner, 1969), chapter 8.
18. H.G. Wells, *The Island of Dr Moreau* (Harmondsworth: Penguin, 1962), p. 86.
19. Ibid., p. 109.
20. Ibid., p. 112.
21. Ibid., p. 118. Other changes in the direction of *The Tempest* included giving the beast-men the opportunity, Caliban-fashion, to express directly to their creator their resentment about the pains that had been taken over them.
22. From John Dryden's Preface to Dryden–Davenant, *The Tempest, or The Enchanted Island* (1670 edn.), A2ᵛ. Available in facsimile in George Robert Guffey (ed.), *After The Tempest* (Los Angeles: University of California Press, 1969).
23. *Motion Picture Herald*, 10 March 1956.

Index

Compiled by Sue Carlton